STOP OVERTHINKING

A Workbook to
CALM YOUR BUSY MIND

MOLLY BURFORD
Author of *The No Worries Workbook*

ADAMS MEDIA

NEW YORK AMSTERDAM/ANTWERP LONDON TORONTO SYDNEY NEW DELHI

Adams Media
An Imprint of Simon & Schuster, LLC
100 Technology Center Drive
Stoughton, Massachusetts 02072

First Adams Media trade paperback edition March 2025

ADAMS MEDIA and colophon are registered trademarks of Simon & Schuster, LLC.

For information about special discounts for bulk purchases, please contact Simon & Schuster Special Sales at 1-866-506-1949 or business@simonandschuster.com.

The Simon & Schuster Speakers Bureau can bring authors to your live event. For more information or to book an event, contact the Simon & Schuster Speakers Bureau at 1-866-248-3049 or visit our website at www.simonspeakers.com.

Interior design by Kellie Emery
Interior images © Adobe Stock/madedee, David, santima.studio, Vilogsign, Natalia, artyway, Миша Герба, Fortuna23, Hendi Harnanto, Hubba Bubba, Pasha, ~Bitter~, zaurrahimov, Tanjilur, Spice, endstern, Екатерина Власенко, lovelymandala, yenaburger, maxicons, Maman

Manufactured in the United States of America

1 2024

ISBN 978-1-5072-2364-2

CONTENTS

INTRODUCTION

Have you ever found yourself frozen when faced with a decision, unable to make one choice over another for fear of "messing up"? Do you find yourself replaying a conversation with a boss, friend, coworker, or even the cashier at the store, hours after the interaction? Or maybe you've been stuck on whether you did the right thing in making that big purchase last month instead of saving the money? Overthinking happens to the very best of us, robbing us of the present moment, our happiness, and our power—but it doesn't have to!

And that's where this workbook comes in. *Stop Overthinking* is filled with more than 120 creative, easy-to-follow activities to help you bring overthinking to a halt and manage your stress in healthier, more productive ways. You will:

- Identify and weed out the root of your overthinking
- Write a personalized self-care checklist
- Beat decision paralysis
- Comfort your inner child
- Practice mindfulness to help ground and center you
- Create a stress-relief playlist
- And more!

You can choose to work through the activities in order, or skip to those that stand out or feel the most helpful in your current overthinking situation. It's all about what works best for *you*.

But before jumping into these activities, be sure to flip through The Basics of Overthinking section on the pages that follow. There you'll explore more about overthinking, learn common signs among those who struggle with this habit, and find out how the creative distractions you'll encounter later in this workbook can help you refocus your mind and quiet racing thoughts.

The biggest thing to keep in mind as you complete this workbook is that overthinking is going to happen—but that doesn't mean it has to control you or dictate your life. You are in the driver's seat. Never forget that. So let's get started!

THE BASICS OF OVERTHINKING

*M*anaging your overthinking starts with understanding it—you need to know exactly *what* overthinking is before you can begin to stop it in its tracks! In the following pages, you'll learn about the basics of overthinking, including possible causes and symptoms, and how creative distractions can help.

What Is Overthinking?

When you have constant and repetitive negative thought cycles about the same thing(s), you are overthinking—also known as ruminating. While everyone has those times of extra stress and worry—they're just part of life—overthinking goes beyond this. Overthinking means incessant, seemingly uncontrollable fixations. It can include obsessing over past mistakes, stressing about the future, or even contemplating a decision to the point that you cannot even make a final choice about what to do. Sound familiar?

Some examples of overthinking include:

- **You went on a first date on Friday night, but now it's Sunday morning and you haven't heard anything from your date.** You thought it went great, but now you're not so sure. As the minutes continue to tick by and no text or call comes through, you start thinking back to the date and try to remember every little detail so you can analyze it at length and figure out how you messed *everything* up.

- **You have an important presentation coming up at work next week.** So naturally, it's all you can think about this week—but not in an excited way. Instead, you feel full of anxiety, constantly revising your Power-Point slides, digging for flaws that might not even exist, and rehearsing your talking points to death. And despite this overpreparation, you don't feel all that ready to present. In fact, the more you prepare, the more tense and full of doubt you feel.
- **You think your best friend is mad at you.** You texted them a few hours ago and have yet to hear back. While no fight or disagreement of any sort ever occurred, you begin going through your text history, trying to figure out if you screwed up and said something that upset them without realizing it.

Overthinking also tends to show up when there's a decision you have to make. The decision can be major: whether or not you should move, find a different job, or get engaged. But sometimes overthinking can apply to a minuscule, everyday choice like what you want to eat for breakfast! In either case, you research your options obsessively, overloading your mind with information and potential outcomes to the point where you can no longer fathom making any choice at all! This is known as analysis and decision paralysis.

Why Is Overthinking So Harmful?

Overthinking is disruptive to your life because it repeatedly takes you out of the present moment and transports you to the land of worst-case scenarios, what-ifs, and doubts. It causes you to freeze up and prevents you from moving forward from the past or taking necessary action now or in the future.

Overthinking can also be mentally and physically *exhausting*. After all, when your mind is in overdrive, that state of hypervigilance drains you of your energy. How could it not? When you're constantly scanning your life for potential threats and bad outcomes, of course you'll be tired! Without the right resources, coping strategies, and support, overthinking can become very difficult to control. In fact, it can feel like *it* is controlling *you*. Because no matter how often someone might try to tell you to just stop thinking about it, it's not that simple.

What Are the Causes of Overthinking?

A lot of different things can lead to overthinking, and overthinking is usually the result of a number of those things building on each other. It's rarely a one-cause problem. Some common elements that can add up to overthinking include:

- **Mental health conditions:** Overthinking can actually be a sign of depression, anxiety, a panic disorder, or post-traumatic stress disorder (PTSD).
- **Trying to control the outcome of a situation:** Overthinking helps give you a sense of control, especially over the uncertain.
- **Stress:** Extra stress—whether it comes from professional, social, or personal sources or elsewhere—can lead to lower defenses against overthinking and make you more prone to mulling over everything going on.
- **Burnout:** If you've been spreading yourself too thin to the point of burnout, overthinking is more likely due to the stress you've been under and the mental exhaustion you're experiencing.
- **Perfectionism:** Perfectionism can make you believe you have to do something perfectly in order to do it at all, and overthinking can feel like a safe alternative to making a mistake.

Again, overthinking is often caused by more than one of these things happening at once. And it can manifest in various ways, which you'll learn more about next.

What Are the Symptoms of Overthinking?

So how do you know when overthinking is becoming an issue? There are many ways overthinking can show up in your day-to-day life, both physically and mentally. The signs to look out for include:

- Difficulty sleeping
- Second-guessing yourself
- Excessive worrying
- Fatigue
- Headaches
- Repetitive thoughts
- Trouble making decisions
- Problems with focusing
- Constant need for reassurance
- Mental exhaustion
- Nausea
- Feeling on edge and/or irritable
- Muscle tension

When overthinking begins to take over your mind, it also takes over your life. Luckily, it can be managed with the right tools, mindsets, and strategies!

The Benefits of Creative Distractions When Overthinking

This workbook uses a creative diversionary approach, which basically just means that you use creative activities to distract yourself from whatever it is you might be overthinking.

Creative distractions can include drawing, coloring, writing, or even decorating or rearranging your home. A creative activity can function as a brain reset button, shifting your attention away from the doom and gloom and back to the present moment. Plus, being creative is just fun!

Creative distractions are great for overthinking for many reasons. They can help to:

- Improve focus
- De-stress
- Reduce negative thoughts
- Enhance mood
- Boost self-esteem
- Strengthen cognition
- And more!

The impact of curbing those racing thoughts with a little creativity can be huge, and now that you know more, it's time to tackle the activities in this workbook!

RATE YOUR CURRENT COPING STRATEGIES

Whether you feel like it or not, you *are* coping with overthinking; you just might not have the best techniques yet. Or maybe some strategies do work well for you at the moment. That's great! However you deal with overthinking, you can use the following table to reflect on your strategies and whether they're helpful when bouts of overthinking strike.

What to Do

In the left-hand column, write down a current coping strategy, and then in the right-hand column give the strategy a rating between 1 and 5 for its effectiveness in helping you feel better, with 1 being completely unhelpful and 5 being super helpful. There's no limit to the potential coping strategies you might list: deep breathing, mindlessly scrolling on Instagram, or crying into your pillow for three hours straight (no judgment here).

Coping Strategy	Rating
_____	1 2 3 4 5
_____	1 2 3 4 5
_____	1 2 3 4 5
_____	1 2 3 4 5

CALL A TRUSTED FRIEND

Calling a good friend can help bring some relief when you're seriously struggling to get out of your own head. Talking to someone you trust will remind you that you're not as alone as you feel, reducing your stress level and inviting you back to a calmer state of mind. You can discuss whatever is weighing on you, or you can try distracting yourself by talking about anything *but* the anxiety.

What to Do

Here, list the people you can turn to when you are overthinking. Then, the next time you find yourself overthinking, use the provided call log. Write down who you talked to, what you talked about, and how you felt before and after the call. If you need help deciding who to call, check out the List Your Support System exercise later in this book.

Call Log — OVERTHINKING EMERGENCY CONTACTS

Who I called:	What we talked about:	How I felt before the call:	How I feel after the call:

PRACTICE POSITIVE SELF-TALK

Shame is a great catalyst for overthinking. When you're not feeling all that great about yourself, repetitive, worrying thoughts can easily pop up. Maybe you feel like you messed up at work, said something silly at a group outing, or did something wrong. In response to these perceived shortcomings, you might engage in negative self-talk (talking to yourself in an unkind manner).

What to Do

It's time to replace your negative self-talk with positive self-talk. Positive self-talk is a means of practicing self-compassion, which is a fantastic way to combat overthinking because it helps you boost your self-esteem, let go of perfectionism, and accept situations as they are.

Using the chart provided, write down your most common negative self-talk phrases and the situations where they tend to pop up. From there, rewrite each phrase to make it compassionate, understanding, and kind. For inspiration, check out these examples:

- "I never do anything right." ⟶ "I do plenty of things right. This is but a blip!"

- "I'm so socially awkward, it's no wonder I'm single." ⟶ "Single is simply a relationship status and reflects nothing about my worth as a person."

- "I'm such a bad employee." ⟶ "I'm doing the best I can with the resources I have."

What Happened	Negative Self-Talk	Positive Self-Talk Rewrite

TAKE A DEEEEEEEP BREATH

Research has shown time and time again that deep breathing works. Not only does deep breathing reduce stress, lessen anxiety, enhance focus, improve depression, and help with sleep, but it also is a great way to reroute overthinking.

What to Do

In this exercise, you're going to practice a technique known as 4-7-8 breathing. This involves taking in a long breath for four seconds, holding that breath for seven seconds, and then releasing it for eight seconds. Repeat the exercise up to four times, until your mind slows down.

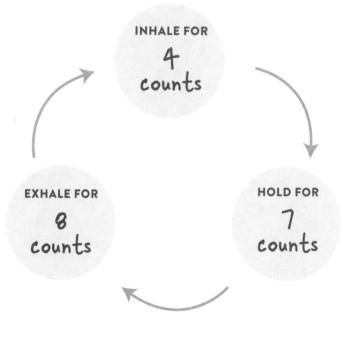

INHALE FOR
4
counts

HOLD FOR
7
counts

EXHALE FOR
8
counts

PRIORITIZE YOUR TASKS

When you have a lot on your to-do list, it's easy to become stuck in the freeze response as you try to determine how you can get everything done. Rome wasn't built in a day, so don't expect yourself to get through everything you need to do in twenty-four hours either! Instead, prioritize your tasks. When you identify what's most important, it becomes easier to defeat task paralysis and keep the ball rolling.

What to Do

In each box, write down one task on your to-do list, when you need it completed, and how long you expect it to take. Then rank each task's urgency level on a scale from 1 to 5 (1 being high priority and 5 being not so urgent). Once you see which tasks are the most urgent, start with those!

Task: _____

    Due date: _____

    How long it will take: _____

    Urgency: _____

Task: _____

    Due date: _____

    How long it will take: _____

    Urgency: _____

Task: _____

    Due date: _____

    How long it will take: _____

    Urgency: _____

Task: _____

    Due date: _____

    How long it will take: _____

    Urgency: _____

BREAK UP WITH YOUR INNER CRITIC

Everyone has an inner critic, and it's more than time to break up with yours. Your inner critic doesn't have your best interests at heart; they actually just want to keep you stuck, insecure, and full of self-doubt.

Your inner critic can cause you to overthink everything, casting self-doubt and worry over everything you've ever done and everything you have yet to do. This is why cutting ties with this toxic character can help you stop overthinking.

What to Do

In the space provided, write a letter to your inner critic and let them know you're breaking up with them—and *why*. Be bold. Be self-respecting. Be honest. Bye, inner critic!

DRAW ONE OF YOUR FAVORITE MEMORIES

Overthinking often shows up as ruminating about painful things that happened in the past. That's why it can be helpful to bring happy memories to the front of your mind. This not only puts things in perspective and helps you remember that life isn't all that bad, but also allows you to practice gratitude. Gratitude can calm your overthinking mind, because it's a mindfulness practice that asks you to focus on the present moment instead of on your own swirling thoughts.

What to Do

Draw one of your favorite memories. You can draw anything, from a fun night out with your best friends to having coffee with your grandma to the day you adopted your dog. All that matters is that the memory brings an immediate smile and helps fill you with a sense of warmth.

TAKE A WALK (AND THEN MEASURE THE RELIEF)

When in doubt, step outdoors and take a nice stroll! Spending time in nature is linked to improved mental health, including lessened anxiety. Walking is also highly beneficial for various reasons, including increased energy levels, strengthened bones, stronger muscles, enhanced cardiovascular health, and more. You can't go wrong with a walk outside!

What to Do

Step away from this workbook for ten to twenty minutes and use that time to go on a walk. Before you do, color in one of the "Before Walk" thermometers with your stress level. When you return, color in the corresponding "After Walk" thermometer. You may notice a change in your stress temperature.

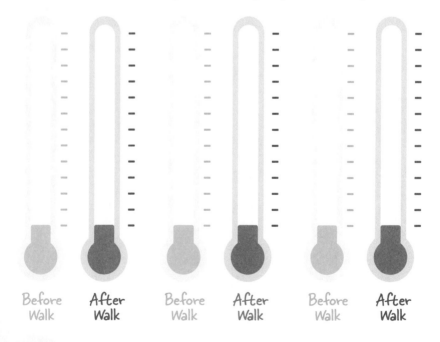

Before Walk · **After Walk** · Before Walk · **After Walk** · Before Walk · **After Walk**

DISTRACT YOURSELF WITH THESE ACTIVITIES

It can be hard to break free from the clutches of an overthinking loop. As you go around and around in circles in your mind, the what-ifs and worry become all you can focus on. Distraction can be an incredibly helpful strategy for defeating overthinking; it takes your attention away from the thought spiral and diverts it elsewhere.

What to Do

Take a look through the provided list of activities, and mark which ones sound appealing to you. Then, the next time overthinking strikes, go and do one!

- ❏ Read a book.
- ❏ Write a short story.
- ❏ Doodle.
- ❏ Clean your room.
- ❏ Reorganize your kitchen drawers.
- ❏ Declutter your closet.
- ❏ Color.
- ❏ Call a friend to ask *them* how they're doing; focus solely on them.
- ❏ Watch your go-to comfort show.
- ❏ Watch the hot new TV series everyone is talking about.
- ❏ Listen to music.
- ❏ Make a new playlist.
- ❏ Watch educational YouTube videos.
- ❏ Take a hot shower.
- ❏ Have a spa day.
- ❏ Bake your favorite dessert.
- ❏ Cook your favorite meal.
- ❏ Journal.

continued on next page

- ❑ Learn a new recipe—or make one up on the fly!
- ❑ Reorganize your bathroom.
- ❑ Offer to help a loved one with something.
- ❑ Knit, crochet, or do another craft that requires you to use your hands.
- ❑ Get cozy with a cup of herbal tea or another warm drink.
- ❑ Go on a long walk.
- ❑ Do a crossword puzzle.
- ❑ Spend time with your pet(s).
- ❑ Volunteer for a cause you're passionate about.

Add your own:

- ❑ _____
- ❑ _____
- ❑ _____
- ❑ _____
- ❑ _____
- ❑ _____
- ❑ _____
- ❑ _____
- ❑ _____
- ❑ _____
- ❑ _____
- ❑ _____
- ❑ _____
- ❑ _____
- ❑ _____

PRACTICE SELF-VALIDATION STATEMENTS

Self-validation is all about establishing trust with yourself through accepting your flaws, acknowledging your strengths, confirming your feelings, and embracing everything you are. Self-validation is great for overcoming overthinking, because it releases your need for perfection, helps regulate your emotions, and increases your self-confidence, all of which are necessary for leaving overthinking behind.

What to Do

Use the following self-validation statements to build trust with yourself. You can recite the statements out loud or silently in your mind—whatever feels best for you. Try repeating each at least three times. Just keep in mind that, if you're used to invalidating yourself, it might feel a little awkward to do the opposite. That's okay; discomfort isn't a sign that this new attitude is wrong. If anything, discomfort is proof that you're growing. Mark the statements that resonate with you the most. If none are speaking to you, that's totally okay; there's space at the end of the list for you to come up with your own!

- I am enough as I am.
- I did the very best I could with the time, resources, and energy I had.
- My feelings matter.
- I am worthy.
- I trust myself.
- I know what I'm doing.
- I am not my mistakes.
- I don't have to be perfect to be loved.
- _____
- _____
- _____

COLOR YOUR WAY TO CALM

Coloring isn't just for kids; it can be a super calming activity for adults too. Coloring is a great distraction because it centers you and forces your mind back into the present moment. Plus, it's fun!

What to Do

Color this charming garden scene. Take your time, play some fun music (your stress-relief playlist, perhaps?), and get lost in the tranquility.

IDENTIFY THE SIGNS YOU'RE OVERGENERALIZING

Cognitive distortions are biased thoughts that can lead to negative thinking and behavioral patterns. Psychologists have identified at least ten different forms of cognitive distortions, but one type that's often a key player in overthinking is overgeneralizing.

When you overgeneralize, you make sweeping assumptions about a situation despite not having a lot of experience or evidence to back up your assumptions. For example, let's say you made a typo in a presentation. When your boss points out your mistake while reviewing the deck, you start beating yourself up and thinking things like "All I ever do is make mistakes. I am the worst employee here. How could I miss something so simple?" Of course, a single typo isn't indicative of your worth at work! But it can seem like the truth in the moment. This is a prime example of overgeneralizing.

What to Do

On the following page, you'll see various road signs, each one labeled with a symptom of overgeneralizing. Do you recognize any of these as behavior you partake in? If so, beneath the road sign, write down how that sign manifests for you.

continued on next page

ASSUMING
THE
WORST

BELIEVING
YOU DO
EVERYTHING
WRONG

_____
_____
_____

_____
_____
_____

USING
THE WORD
"NEVER"
OR
"ALWAYS"

DEFINING
YOURSELF
BY ONE
MISTAKE

_____
_____
_____

_____
_____
_____

NEGATIVE
SELF-TALK

_____
_____
_____

NEUTRALIZE YOUR ANXIOUS THOUGHTS

When overthinking manifests as anxious thoughts, you can neutralize it by reminding yourself that a thought is just a thought and is not always reflective of reality. By detaching yourself from your thoughts, you become able to let go of them and take their power away.

What to Do

Write down the narrative that goes through your mind when you're having anxious thoughts. For example: "I'm so worried my best friend is mad at me, because I double-texted and she still hasn't replied so now she probably thinks I'm the most annoying human being alive." Once you have the thought on paper, rewrite it from a place of observant detachment. For example: "My worry about my BFF hating me is just a thought and probably not rooted in reality. She is most likely not replying to my texts because she is busy."

Neutralization #1
- The anxious thought: _____
- The detached, observant thought: _____

Neutralization #2
- The anxious thought: _____
- The detached, observant thought: _____

Neutralization #3
- The anxious thought: _____
- The detached, observant thought: _____

STOP "SHOULDING" ON YOURSELF

"Should" statements are a type of cognitive distortion that can lead to rigid thinking as you create hard rules for yourself. For example: "I should make my bed every single morning so I can have the most productive day possible."

While you may believe this thought is motivating, there are going to be chaotic days when making your bed just isn't a practical option. However, if you have constantly told yourself that making your bed is a nonnegotiable, falling short of your self-imposed rule will make you feel lazy or like a total failure.

What to Do

In the space provided, write down your most common should statements, and then remove the absolute phrasing from them. For example, the previous statement about making your bed can be turned into something like "If I have the time, I like to make my bed in the morning before leaving for work. I understand life happens and this won't always be possible. I trust myself to know when I have time."

Remove the Should

- Should statement: _____
- Rewrite: _____

Remove the Should

- Should statement: _____
- Rewrite: _____

Remove the Should

- Should statement: _____
- Rewrite: _____

TRY PROGRESSIVE MUSCLE RELAXATION

Progressive muscle relaxation is an exercise that brings you back into your body as you focus on tensing and then relaxing one part of your body at a time. It is linked to a host of benefits, including decreased anxiety and stress levels, improved sleep quality, lowered blood pressure, and reduced physical pain.

What to Do

Performing progressive muscle relaxation is easy! All you need is ten to fifteen minutes to yourself and a quiet area. (Pro tip: You can also do mini bouts of progressive muscle relaxation at your desk if you're stressing at the office; no one will ever know!)

First, get into a comfortable position. You can sit upright in a comfy chair or lie on the floor. From there, focus on one individual body part at a time, tensing and then relaxing the muscles of each part in turn. As you release, feel your worries melt away.

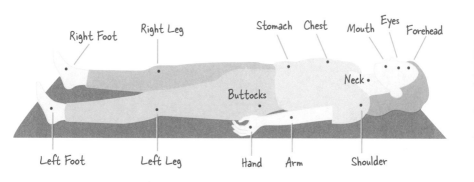

LIST YOUR STRENGTHS

Overthinking can diminish your self-esteem and make you forget how strong you truly are. The truth is you are much more powerful than you're likely giving yourself credit for being. You have so much to offer and tons of potential!

What to Do

List your strengths to remind yourself of your worth, your capabilities, and your power.

1. _____
2. _____
3. _____
4. _____
5. _____
6. _____
7. _____
8. _____
9. _____
10. _____
11. _____
12. _____
13. _____
14. _____
15. _____
16. _____

OWN YOUR WEAKNESSES

You're human, which means you are imperfect by design. But that's part of the fun of being alive! And ultimately your weaknesses are part of what makes you, well, *you*. Acknowledging your imperfections takes power away from them and puts it back in your hands.

What to Do

Fill in the blanks to own your shortcomings:

- I am _____, but that's okay.
- I struggle with _____, but that's okay.
- I wish I were better at _____, but that's okay.
- I wish I had done _____ differently, but that's okay.
- I feel bad about _____, but that's okay.

WORK THROUGH THE WORST-CASE SCENARIO

Worried about something going terribly wrong in the future? Maybe going on a horrible first date? Missing an important deadline at work? Embarrassing yourself at a birthday party? General calamity at the upcoming family function? Whatever it may be, it really is going to be okay, even if the worst-case scenario comes true. And you know why? Because you'll be prepared to handle it after doing this exercise!

Working through the worst-case scenario will help you stop overthinking, because it will help you feel more confidence in yourself when it comes to handling any problems that might arise. After you think through the worst-case scenario, you'll be ready to put the potential disaster on the metaphorical shelf and move on with your day. After all, if anything goes south, you've got it handled!

What to Do

Name the situation in question and what you believe its worst-case scenario to be. From there, brainstorm ways to cope with the fallout. Also, list anyone who could support you, along with any strengths of yours that could come in handy in the scenario. Finally, come up with a comforting affirmation you can repeat to yourself whenever you find your thoughts jumping to the worst (for example, "It's going to be okay, even if my first date doesn't go smoothly").

The Situation:

_____

_____

The Worst-Case Scenario:

_____

_____

What I Can Do If It Happens:

_____

_____

Who I Can Get Help from:

_____

_____

My Strengths:

_____

_____

Comforting Affirmation:

_____

_____

CONSIDER THE *BEST-CASE* SCENARIO

Things really can (and often do) work in your favor! Or, at the very least, things can turn out better than you may have expected. And sure, hoping for the best doesn't guarantee it will happen. But remember that worrying about the worst doesn't make *that* come true either. Operating from a hopeful, more positive place is better for your mental health than worrying.

What to Do

It's time to flip that catastrophic thinking on its head by considering the best-case scenario. Here, write down current anxiety-inducing situations and then imagine their best-case scenarios. For example, the job interview you're spiraling about actually goes so well that you get the job! Or the first date leads to a second because you two vibed so much. Dream big here! What's the best that can happen?

Best Case #1

- The situation: _____
- The best-case scenario: _____

Best Case #2

- The situation: _____
- The best-case scenario: _____

Best Case #3

- The situation: _____
- The best-case scenario: _____

DRAW HEALTHY BOUNDARIES

Boundaries are *essential* for your well-being, because they keep you safe. They help you prioritize your time and what is most important and beneficial for you. You can set boundaries with just yourself, with the people in your life, with your job, and more. You might set boundaries about when you're available to be reached by phone, whether you'll answer professional emails outside of work hours, which subjects you're willing to discuss with family members, or whom you'll text (for example, not your ex).

What to Do

Here, draw a picture of yourself on one side of the fence. On the other side of the fence, write down your boundaries and why you need them.

DETACH FROM THE OUTCOME

Overthinking can arise when you're trying to be in control of something, like how a friend will react when you tell them about something.

The bad news: You can't *really* control *any* outcome.
The good news: You *can* control your own actions in this moment!

When you get attached to a specific outcome, you can become so busy overthinking about the result that you don't consider the present actions you can take. For example, maybe you want to save an emergency fund of $1,000. You become so focused on that large dollar amount that you become overwhelmed by how far you have to go. Instead of feeling defeated by the journey and how long it might take, think about something you can do today (for example, cooking at home instead of ordering delivery) that would get you that much closer to your savings goal.

What to Do

The future isn't within your control; you can only control your own actions right here, in the present moment. Work on detaching from the outcome by using the following space to write about what you want to happen and then brainstorming what you can do *right now* to move toward the outcome you hope for.

TIME BLOCK YOUR DAY

When life gets busy, as it often does, it's easy to become overwhelmed with everything on your plate. It truly can feel as though there will never be enough hours in the day to get everything done!

While you can't create more time, you can manage it more effectively through time blocking. That means breaking up your day into smaller chunks of time, then dedicating each block to a specific task (or group of tasks).

Time blocking can help with overthinking because it stops the cycle of guesswork about how you can possibly get everything done. It helps you just get started.

What to Do

On a hectic day when your to-do list is longer than a convenience store receipt, turn to this time-block chart and use it to plan out your day. You can re-create the chart on a separate piece of paper whenever your to-do list feels overwhelming.

Time	Task

LEARN FROM YOUR MISTAKES

Mistakes happen. That's just part of being human. Not one person gets it right every single time, and this is what makes this life interesting and dynamic. Perfection is boring!

That said, when you're in the midst of a mistake, it's not fun. It can feel embarrassing, painful, or shame-inducing. So, in an attempt to protect your ego and feel less out of control, you might begin overthinking what you could have done differently to avoid this mess in the first place.

Instead of obsessing over the mistake, shift your focus to the lesson that can be learned from the experience.

What to Do

Reflect on mistakes you've made, and then determine what you learned from them.

Helpful Mistake #1

- The mistake: _____
- The lesson: _____

Helpful Mistake #2

- The mistake: _____
- The lesson: _____

Helpful Mistake #3

- The mistake: _____
- The lesson: _____

Helpful Mistake #4

- The mistake:
- The lesson:

Helpful Mistake #5

- The mistake:
- The lesson:

Helpful Mistake #6

- The mistake:
- The lesson:

Helpful Mistake #7

- The mistake:
- The lesson:

Helpful Mistake #8

- The mistake:
- The lesson:

Helpful Mistake #9

- The mistake:
- The lesson:

NAME THE GREATEST HITS (OVERTHINKING'S VERSION)

Just as catchy TikTok songs get stuck in your head, the same thoughts play on repeat in your mind too. This is because overthinking tends to follow the well-worn paths of your greatest fears and deepest vulnerabilities.

For example, perhaps an upcoming interview for a new job is throwing you into a full-blown spiral because you want the position *so* badly that you are afraid of what it will say about you and your worth if you *aren't* offered the role. Those thoughts may have much more to do with your own fears than with what a job offer (or lack of one) would actually signify.

Whatever your most common thoughts are when overthinking, by noticing the pattern, you can help stop future bouts of overthinking right in their tracks. You can recognize a thought as just that—overthinking—and not as a reflection of reality. And once you realize you're overthinking, you can turn to coping strategies to help ground you. Basically, you're able to hit pause on a meltdown and instead enjoy the melody of serenity!

What to Do

To help you easily identify common overthinking triggers, name and create album covers for your greatest overthinking hits. On the following page, title each blank album cover with a thought that plays on repeat in your mind. For example: "Everyone in the Group Chat Hates Me," "I Shouldn't Have Told That Weird Joke in 2008," and "I'm Going to Fail My Exam." For album art, draw whatever comes to mind about that particular greatest hit.

DRAW YOUR WAY TO CALM

Doing something creative such as drawing is a wonderful way to distract yourself from overthinking. Remember, you don't have to be an amazing artist to enjoy this activity and find it helpful! The point is to express yourself, release stress, and take a break.

What to Do

Draw the most calming scene you can think of. This could be the beach, a forest, a waterfall, a garden with stunning flowers—whatever makes you feel peaceful.

CREATE A STRESS-RELIEF PLAYLIST

Music is known to be excellent for stress relief. It can help center you and calm you down. Plus, your favorite songs can also be a huge source of comfort during stressful times!

What to Do

On the screen provided, write down some of the most relaxing songs you know and love. Once you've brainstormed a bit, add those songs to a playlist on your preferred music streaming service so you can turn to them whenever overthinking comes around!

IMPROVE YOUR SELF-TRUST

Fostering self-trust can help with overthinking, because it quiets second-guessing, increases your confidence in your choices, and improves your self-esteem. One way to build your self-trust is by making small, attainable promises to yourself—for example, "I won't turn on the TV tonight until after I work out" or "I am going to take the trash out after dinner." In making small commitments and fulfilling them, you will gradually learn to trust yourself more.

What to Do

Write down some small promises you can make to yourself, and then reflect on the outcome. Look through the provided examples to get inspired!

I Promise . . .

- The self-promise: I will go to the gym three times this week for thirty minutes at a time.
- Date(s) completed: Monday, Tuesday, and Saturday.
- How I feel afterward: Sore but proud!

I Promise . . .

- The self-promise: I won't text my ex on their birthday.
- Date(s) completed: Their birthday.
- How I feel afterward: Self-respecting! Empowered! Great!

I Promise . . .

- The self-promise: _____
- Date(s) completed: _____
- How I feel afterward: _____

I Promise . . .

- The self-promise: _____
- Date(s) completed: _____
- How I feel afterward: _____

I Promise . . .

- The self-promise: _____
- Date(s) completed: _____
- How I feel afterward: _____

I Promise . . .

- The self-promise: _____
- Date(s) completed: _____
- How I feel afterward: _____

I Promise . . .

- The self-promise: _____
- Date(s) completed: _____
- How I feel afterward: _____

I Promise . . .

- The self-promise: _____
- Date(s) completed: _____
- How I feel afterward: _____

LIST YOUR SUPPORT SYSTEM

Many, many people are rooting for you and have your back, and this is important to keep in mind, especially when you're overthinking. When you're stuck in your own head and mulling over your problems, mess-ups, and worst-case scenarios, it's easy to feel completely alone. It can be difficult to reach out for help; you might be embarrassed about the situation at hand, or maybe you're just convinced that no one would ever understand.

Here's the thing, though: You *do* deserve support, and you might even be surprised to learn that other people can be much more understanding than your anxious mind is giving them credit for. In this exercise, you're going to remind yourself of who will be there for you when tough times strike.

What to Do

Write about your support system. Include each supportive person's name, your relationship to them, and how they support you. For example, your sister, Sarah, might be an awesome listener for love-life issues while your dad, Tim, is super helpful when it comes to problem-solving issues going on within your career.

Support #1

- Name: _____
- Relationship: _____
- How they support me: _____

Support #2

- Name: _____
- Relationship: _____
- How they support me: _____

Support #3

- Name: _____

- Relationship: _____

- How they support me: _____

Support #4

- Name: _____

- Relationship: _____

- How they support me: _____

Support #5

- Name: _____

- Relationship: _____

- How they support me: _____

Support #6

- Name: _____

- Relationship: _____

- How they support me: _____

CHALLENGE YOUR TOXIC CORE BELIEFS

Core beliefs are ideas that shape the way you see the world, other people, yourself, and your life as a whole. While some core beliefs are productive, you might have others that hold you back and keep you stuck in unhealthy situations, mindsets, and behavioral patterns.

Some examples of common toxic core beliefs include:

- I'm not good enough.
- People can't be trusted.
- The world is a bad and broken place.

What to Do

Write down your toxic core beliefs, and then challenge them. You can challenge them by reframing them, or by listing evidence to the contrary. For example, "I will never find love" can be changed to "Love is taking a little longer than I would like, but that's okay. A relationship will never define my worth."

Challenging My Beliefs #1

- Toxic core belief: _____
- Challenge: _____

Challenging My Beliefs #2

- Toxic core belief: _____
- Challenge: _____

Challenging My Beliefs #3

- Toxic core belief: _____
- Challenge: _____

NAME THE PROS AND CONS AND MAKE A BIG, SCARY DECISION

If you have a major decision on the horizon and are in full-blown panic mode, it can be hard to know what to do. This is where naming the pros and cons of a possible path can be helpful.

What to Do

On the following page, list the pros and cons of an action you're considering. For example, let's say you're thinking about saying yes to a new job. A pro would be an *amazing* pay raise. A con would be the awkward conversation with your current boss about quitting. Looking at the pro and con side by side, it's clear that taking the new job would probably be the most beneficial for you.

After you're done listing the pros and cons, in the space provided, write down your decision and why you're making it.

continued on next page

Pros	Cons

My Decision

DISMISS THE SECOND GUESS

Second-guessing is one of the biggest signs you're overthinking. Maybe after you've committed to a decision, instead of moving forward confidently, you worry over whether you made the wrong choice. Or maybe you flip-flop endlessly about an upcoming decision you need to make.

Second-guessing can happen with decisions large and small, from what you're going to wear to work to whether you should break up with your partner.

What to Do

First, get in a comfortable position, either sitting or lying down, and then close your eyes. While breathing in and out slowly, envision your second guess as a balloon. Now, picture yourself popping that balloon. Repeat this a few times until the second guess is nothing but a fading memory.

SET A TEN-MINUTE TIMER FOR A LIL FREAK-OUT

Sometimes, you just need a good, old-fashioned meltdown before you can move on from something. However, your freak-out shouldn't consume your entire day.

What to Do

Set a ten-minute timer on your phone and let yourself ruminate to your heart's content. Once the timer goes off, you must completely stop. Ready? Freak out!

SELF-SOOTHE WITH THESE METHODS

While you're never truly alone, sometimes you have to be your own best friend. For example, maybe it's 2 a.m. and no one is awake to consult about a choice, meaning you need to make it all on your own. If this is your predicament, that's okay. There are so many ways you can show up for yourself and put your own mind at ease.

Calming down on your own is also known as self-soothing. And there's a wide range of actions and techniques that can help you to regulate your emotions solo.

What to Do

Keep in mind that some self-soothing techniques will work better for you than for others and vice versa. This is normal; we're all different, and we all have different needs! If you find particular self-soothing strategies on this list helpful, make sure to mark them so you can return to them whenever you need to.

- Change your physical location (i.e., if you're in your bedroom, go to your kitchen).
- Take a warm shower or bath.
- Light a candle and breathe in its scent.
- Put on a diffuser.
- Make a cup of coffee or tea, and then drink it mindfully.
- Watch ASMR videos on YouTube.
- Put on relaxing music.
- Do a yoga flow.
- Journal.
- Stretch.
- Practice deep breathing.
- Go on a leisurely walk.
- Do a vigorous exercise.
- Shake it off by putting on upbeat music and dancing.
- Lie down for ten minutes.
- Meditate.

BRAIN DUMP HERE!

Sometimes, just getting everything you're stressing about out of your head and onto a page can be wildly helpful in making all those anxious thoughts feel less jumbled and scary. Later in this book, there are a couple of other brain dump pages like this one. Turn to them whenever the need to vent arises.

What to Do

Use this page in whatever way makes the most sense to *you*. There's no right or wrong way to brain dump.

PLAN A DIFFICULT CONVERSATION

Even the happiest and healthiest of relationships have conflicts; in fact, conflict is a natural part of connecting to other people. Plus, conflict can be healthy, as it's better to talk things through than hold it all in (that's how resentment happens and how problems become bigger).

That said, confrontation is not easy, *especially* when you're an overthinker. Whether a friend crossed a boundary or a family member hurt your feelings, problems can be difficult to bring up and talk through. However, planning ahead for a potentially awkward discussion can help you feel more grounded, confident, and secure going in. Plus, calm preparation can help you stay focused when you're having the conversation.

What to Do

Use this chart to plan out difficult conversations. Include who you need to talk to, why, and what you want the outcome to be.

Who	Why	Desired Outcome

SHIFT YOUR FOCUS

Perspective really is everything, and sometimes yours may become skewed due to overthinking. This is why *shifting* your focus is such a good way to curb those racing, worried thoughts.

What to Do

On the following page, draw what you're currently overthinking about on the left-hand side. As you draw, think about how this focus is negatively impacting you. Then, on the right-hand side, draw this situation in a different light. So, for example, if you're overthinking a text you sent to a friend, draw a phone screen with the message you wrote on the left-hand side. On the right-hand side of the page, draw a positive response from your friend.

COLOR YOUR WAY TO INNER PEACE

Grab your colored pencils, crayons, or markers—it's coloring time!

What to Do

Color in the koi pond. Do your best to focus only on the act of coloring. Maybe put your phone on Do Not Disturb and block out any other distractions. Be completely in the moment.

USE THE TWO-MINUTE RULE TO BEAT PROCRASTINATION

When you're overthinking what you need to start with on a busy day, turn to the two-minute rule. Created by productivity expert David Allen (originator of the Getting Things Done workflow management method), this rule can help you push your worries aside and just get started.

What to Do

The two-minute rule is simple: If you can complete a task in two minutes or less, you should just do it immediately instead of putting it off. Here, write a short to-do list of two-minute tasks you're stressing about. Once you have your list, get going. You've got this!

In under two minutes I can:

❑ _____

❑ _____

❑ _____

❑ _____

❑ _____

-02:00-

BE CURIOUS (NOT FEARFUL) ABOUT THE FUTURE

Yes, the future can be scary. After all, you can't predict what's going to happen—it's uncharted territory. This fact can be anxiety-inducing because it means *anything* can happen, good *or* bad.

However, instead of being afraid of what could happen, try to be curious, even about potentially frustrating experiences. Curiosity is essentially a practice in gratitude, which is helpful for bringing you back to the present and away from your overactive mind.

What to Do

On the following page, write about your curiosity about what could happen. Consider lessons you could learn, people you could meet, and other possibilities of all kinds.

I am curious about the future because . . .

PERFORM THE FIVE SENSES MEDITATION

Because overthinking takes you out of the present, grounding exercises can be incredibly helpful for bringing you back to the moment at hand. One great technique is known as the five senses meditation. This meditation uses the five senses—sight, touch, sound, smell, and taste—to soothe anxiety. The great thing about the five senses meditation is that you can do it anywhere!

What to Do

Follow these steps to perform the five senses meditation:

1. **Sight:** Name five things you can see in your immediate surroundings. Really look at each one, observing its color, texture, size, and shape.
2. **Touch:** Next, name four things you can physically feel—for example, the back of the chair you're sitting on, the table you're resting your elbow on, or your hair on the back of your neck.
3. **Sound:** Now take a deep breath in and name three things you can hear. Be mindful about where each sound is coming from.
4. **Smell:** Name two things you can smell.
5. **Taste:** Finally, name one thing you can taste, such as the minty toothpaste you brushed your teeth with this morning or the coffee you just drank.

VISUALIZE CALMING OCEAN WAVES

Visualization is a meditation technique used to help recenter and de-stress. If you're in an overthinking spiral, using visualization is a great way to tune out the mental noise and feel calmer.

What to Do

For this particular visualization exercise, you're going to imagine ocean waves lapping up on a shore.

1. Take a deep breath and close your eyes.
2. Now picture sitting on an ocean beach. It can be a beach you've visited before or one you've made up in your mind.
3. As you imagine the beach, describe to yourself what you're experiencing. For example: "I feel the sun warming my shoulders, a breeze rustling my hair. There is sand between my toes."
4. As you sink into the scene in your mind, divert your attention to the ocean's waves. Focus on their motion, their speed, and the way they work at the sand along the shoreline.
5. Keep focusing on this beach scene for at least five minutes or until you feel calmer.

Tip: For extra help, during these steps, play calming ocean sounds on YouTube, Spotify, or whichever streaming service you use.

WRITE SELF-FORGIVENESS STATEMENTS

A fact: You're human. Another fact: This means you're *going* to mess up, because humans aren't perfect. But that's okay! It makes us more interesting and complex beings, right?

However, in practice, it can be difficult to make room for your humanity and allow for mistakes. Often, like many of us, you aim for perfection instead. So when you (inevitably) fall short of that ten-out-of-ten score you were aiming for, it's only natural to succumb to the dreaded overthinking spiral of doom. This is where self-forgiveness comes into play.

What to Do

Use the following template to practice forgiving yourself for mistakes you can't stop overthinking. Acknowledge what you did and also what you wish you had done differently, and then write accompanying self-forgiveness statements about whatever your regret(s) may be.

For example, let's say you arrived late to meet a friend for a concert and now they're annoyed with you. You could write, "I wish I had given my friend more of a heads-up about traffic and that I would be fifteen minutes late. But I have to keep in mind I was trying to drive safely and did my best. Next time, I will give a more accurate ETA so I don't leave anyone hanging. I forgive myself and give myself permission to learn from this mistake instead of hanging on to it."

Self-Forgiveness #1

- What happened: _____
- What I did (and why): _____
- What I wish I'd done differently (and why): _____
- How I can do better next time: _____

Self-Forgiveness #2

- What happened: _____
- What I did (and why): _____
- What I wish I'd done differently (and why): _____
- How I can do better next time: _____

Self-Forgiveness #3

- What happened: _____
- What I did (and why): _____
- What I wish I'd done differently (and why): _____
- How I can do better next time: _____

Self-Forgiveness #4

- What happened: _____
- What I did (and why): _____
- What I wish I'd done differently (and why): _____
- How I can do better next time: _____

Self-Forgiveness #5

- What happened: _____
- What I did (and why): _____
- What I wish I'd done differently (and why): _____
- How I can do better next time: _____

RECITE RADICAL ACCEPTANCE STATEMENTS

The concept of radical acceptance has roots in Buddhism and is used in dialectical behavioral therapy (DBT). Radical acceptance asks you to completely accept a situation as it is, without judgment or resistance. Radical acceptance doesn't mean you have to love whatever is going on; it just means you take it as all that it is.

Radical acceptance is often practiced through repeating coping statements such as:

- It is what it is.
- I can't change what has already happened.
- I can't predict the future.
- I can tolerate discomfort.
- I can choose to respond differently next time.

Radical acceptance can soothe overthinking by reminding you that you *can* get through difficult situations. It helps you respond to tough events with empowerment and realistic expectations and gives you permission to detach from and let go of what has already happened.

What to Do

Write out a few radical acceptance statements you can turn to when needed. Choose from the examples listed previously, or write your own:

1. _____

2. _____

3. _____

TAKE YOUR STRESS-LEVEL TEMPERATURE

Overthinking is often the result of stress, which is why being aware of your current stress level is helpful for coping with overthinking. If you realize you're headed for a freak-out, you can take the steps to calm down and bring your stress level back to normal.

What to Do

Color the thermometer to represent your current stress level. When you're done, in the provided lines, write about what is going on in your life right now and see what could be contributing to your current state of stress.

— Breaking Point

—

— SOS

—

— Aaargh!

—

— Tense

—

— Stressed but Overall Fine

—

— Calm and Collected

DELEGATE WHAT YOU CAN

You don't have to do everything on your own. No, seriously: You *really* don't. If you're hesitant to ask for a hand because you don't want to be a burden or seem weak, please know that asking for help is neither a sign of weakness nor does it make you a burden. Everyone needs help every now and then, and that's just fine.

What to Do

List your current responsibilities and determine which ones you can seek assistance with. Write down who can help you with those tasks and how. For example, maybe your sister can help you put together your new furniture, your partner can give you a ride to the airport, or your friend can help you organize your closet.

Current Responsibilities/To-Dos:

1. _____
2. _____
3. _____
4. _____
5. _____
6. _____
7. _____
8. _____
9. _____
10. _____

Who can help and how:

DO BOX BREATHING

Box breathing, also known as 4-4-4-4 or square breathing, is an awesome technique to help calm an overactive mind and recenter yourself.

What to Do

Box breathing is easy—just follow these steps:

1. Find a comfortable chair to sit on. Make sure your back is touching the back of the chair and your feet are flat on the floor.
2. Close your eyes.
3. For four counts, slowly inhale through your nose.
4. Hold this breath for four counts.
5. Release this breath through your mouth for four counts.
6. Hold your exhale for another four counts.
7. Repeat these steps one to three times, until you feel calmer and more at ease.

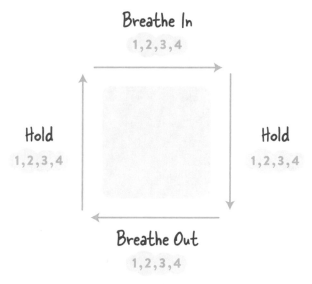

Breathe In
1,2,3,4

Hold
1,2,3,4

Hold
1,2,3,4

Breathe Out
1,2,3,4

RELEASE PERFECTIONISM

Overthinking can happen when you want to be perfect. Perfectionism puts a lot of unnecessary pressure on a person. After all, no one is perfect, and no one ever will be! It's an unfair bar to aspire to.

What to Do

In this exercise, you're going to visualize dismissing perfectionism. First, get in a comfortable position and close your eyes. Then take a few deep breaths—in through your nose and out through your mouth. Once you're feeling calmer, clench your fists for five seconds. After five seconds, release your fingers, uncurling them slowly. As you do this, recite the following affirmation: "I release the need to be perfect." Repeat these steps three or four times, until you feel your thoughts slowing and your mind relaxing.

UNDERSTAND YOUR LOCUS OF CONTROL

"Locus" means "place," and your locus of control is where you believe the events in your life originate, or how much power you have over what happens to you.

If you have an internal locus of control, you believe you can control what happens. If your locus of control is external, you think events and forces outside yourself are in charge of what goes on. Most people operate from somewhere in between these two extremes, and a person's locus of control can shift over time.

Knowing what type of locus of control you're working from, and whether it's a truly accurate gauge of the situation, can help you stop overthinking, because it can move your focus to what truly is in your hands (and what isn't).

What to Do

With a specific problem you're currently overthinking in mind, fill out the prompts on the next page to identify and reflect on the locus of control you're working from.

What am I overthinking?

What story am I telling myself about this issue?

In this story, what or who do I assume has the power to change the outcome?

Are these assumptions accurate? Why or why not?

What, if anything, can I control?

What, if anything, is out of my control?

BRAIN DUMP HERE!

Another brain dump session!

What to Do

All you need to do here is write down everything that's on your mind. It doesn't have to have any structure, rhyme, or reason. It's about getting all your thoughts out of your mind and onto the page. Go ahead!

GET A REALITY CHECK

A quick reality check can help you stop and focus on what is actually true about a stressful thought or event. This skill is often used in dialectical behavioral therapy (DBT), a form of therapy based on mindfulness, where it's called "checking the facts."

What to Do

Check the facts on what you are currently overthinking with these prompts:

- What emotion do I want to change?

- What prompted this feeling?

- What am I thinking, assuming, or interpreting about this event?

- What are other ways to view this situation?

- Do I think there is a threat?

- How likely is it to happen?

- What is the worst thing that could happen?

- Is my emotional response aligned with what is happening?

REFRAME THE STRESSFUL SITUATION

Distressing things happen. This is an unavoidable fact of life. However, obsessing over the negative doesn't make it better; in fact, it makes the pain and discomfort far worse. This is where reframing can be helpful. Reframing is looking at something painful or anxiety-inducing through a different lens. For example, let's say you just had a fight with your best friend. You might be replaying everything you think you said "wrong" during the argument and worrying that they will never want to be your friend again. Your current viewpoint might be something along the lines of, "Ugh, I shouldn't have lost my cool like that. Now they definitely hate me. I am a horrible friend, and I don't deserve love." To reframe your viewpoint to be not only more grounded in reality but also more compassionate toward yourself, you could think, "I feel guilty for getting so upset with a friend I care about so dearly. I know she still loves me, and that fights happen. It's going to be okay."

Research has shown that using reframing strategies is an effective way to manage stress because it can change your physical and mental response to stressors.

What to Do

In the "Stressful Sitch" frame, draw the event you're ruminating over, and write a caption for your drawing. Then reframe the event in the "The Reframe" frame and write a caption for that drawing. For example, let's say you made a typo in a presentation deck at work and you didn't catch it . . . until you were presenting it in front of your boss and coworkers. Draw the memory in the "Stressful Sitch" frame and caption it "How could I have screwed that up?" Then, in the "The Reframe" frame, draw yourself calm and caption it "I made a mistake but that doesn't define my worth. I can be more careful next time."

Stressful Sitch

The Reframe

Stressful Sitch

The Reframe

Stressful Sitch

The Reframe

CREATE YOUR CALM TOOLBOX

During stressful times, it can be hard to keep your cool. This is why having some tools at the ready for anxious moments can help you make it through in one piece.

What to Do

Inside the toolbox, draw the things that calm you down, labeling each one. For example, you could draw your dog if you have one, or your favorite candle, or a table set for dinner with your best friend, or a cup of tea. Turn to this page in moments of overthinking so you can be reminded of what helps.

NOTICE YOUR SELF-LIMITING BELIEFS

Self-limiting beliefs are ideas you have about yourself that prevent you from living up to your fullest potential. They're similar to toxic core beliefs, but they're specifically about yourself rather than about life in general. Many times, self-limiting beliefs are subconscious and you barely notice them. However, that doesn't mean they aren't powerful.

Self-limiting beliefs have many negative consequences, including imposter syndrome, anxiety, and procrastination. Some examples of common limiting beliefs include:

- "I'm not good enough."
- "It's too late for me to change."
- "I'm never going to find a partner."
- "I don't deserve a better job. I should just stay put."

What to Do

Reflect on some of your own self-limiting beliefs, and write them down in the blank space provided. Once you have your list, challenge those beliefs. You can do this by rewriting them to be more positive or by listing evidence that shows them to be inaccurate.

Self-limiting beliefs:

- _____
- _____
- _____

Challenge:

- _____
- _____
- _____

IMPROVE YOUR SLEEP HYGIENE

Lacking in the sleep department makes you much more vulnerable to over-thinking. In fact, spending an inadequate amount of time in bed has negative impacts on your mental *and* physical health, including increased anxiety; worsened depression; irritability; and a higher risk of heart disease, diabetes, accidents, hypertension, and more. Getting enough sleep can improve your mood, reduce stress, lower your risk of heart disease, enhance your decision-making and problem-solving skills, increase your attention span, strengthen your immune system, and more.

If you constantly feel tired and burned out, there's a good chance you need to work on your sleep hygiene—the quality of your sleep routine.

What to Do

Try the following sleep hygiene methods for at least one week. For each one you try, write about what you noticed.

- Get seven to eight hours of sleep per night.
- Do not use electronics before bed.
- Do not consume coffee or other caffeinated beverages after 2 p.m.
- Do not consume alcohol close to bedtime.
- Wake up and go to bed at the same times every single day.

Day	Sleep Hygiene	Notes
Monday		
Tuesday		
Wednesday		
Thursday		
Friday		
Saturday		
Sunday		

BEAT DECISION PARALYSIS

When a decision needs to be made, big or small, overthinking loves to creep right in and share its many, *many* thoughts with you. This can lead to second-guessing, overwhelm, and eventually freezing instead of making a choice.

Oftentimes, this is because you're so afraid of making the "wrong" decision that you'd honestly rather not act at all. Other times, it might be because you're terrified of being judged by others for whatever choice you might make.

In any event, you can't avoid making choices in life. You need to step into your power and learn to trust your instincts. You know what to do! The cloud of overthinking is simply getting in the way.

What to Do

In this activity, you're going to beat decision paralysis by following these steps:

1. Set an appropriate decision deadline: _____

2. Be honest: Why are you so afraid of making this decision? _____

   _____

3. What is your gut choice? _____

4. Why is it your gut choice? _____

5. Make the official decision and write it here: _____

PLAN A RESET HOUR

When your head is spinning with what-ifs, worst-case scenarios, and general doom, it can be hard to get a grip. This is why a reset hour can help bring you back to earth and make you feel ready to deal with everything you have going on.

What to Do

Write down everything you feel is in disarray. For example, maybe your kitchen has dishes stacked up in the sink, your bed is unmade, you haven't checked the mail in four days, etc.

_____

_____

_____

Once you have your list, set a timer for one hour and take care of as many items on your list as possible. Once the timer goes off, you can give yourself permission to stop and move on with your day in a clearer headspace.

CHANGE THE CHANNEL

Overthinking isn't just exhausting and unproductive; it gets annoying after a while! It's like watching reruns of the same (bad) show over and over and over again. That's where this visualization exercise comes into play. You're going to literally switch away from the overthinking channel in your mind and start watching something better.

What to Do

Follow these steps to change the channel from overthinking:

1. Close your eyes and visualize yourself watching TV. Imagine that the thing you're overthinking is the show you've tuned into.
2. As you feel yourself getting irritated by this programming, picture yourself reaching over to the coffee table and grabbing the remote.
3. Change the channel to view a happy memory. Picture it playing out on the screen in detail.
4. As you watch the better times, focus on how you feel.
5. If you notice an urge to change the channel back to the rumination programming, gently invite yourself back to the moment you're remembering on the screen.
6. Perform this exercise until you feel a sense of calm wash over you. Then, open your eyes and move on with your day!

CULTIVATE SELF-COMPASSION WITH MEDITATION

Self-compassion is key to living a more fulfilling life. It's also great to turn to when bouts of overthinking happen, particularly when you're overthinking a mistake or a social faux pas or are generally spiraling in self-loathing.

Practicing self-compassion is linked to many great benefits, including less reactivity to fear, greater resilience, and a higher tolerance for imperfection, all of which are helpful things when overthinking is taking over your brain.

What to Do

To cultivate self-compassion, perform a meditation known as the loving-kindness meditation. Follow these steps:

1. Find a comfortable space where you can sit or lie down.
2. Close your eyes and bring your attention to your breath. Notice its pace and whether you're breathing mostly through your nose or mouth.
3. Begin to breathe more deeply and intentionally in through your nose and out through your mouth. Regulate your breathing to a pace that's comfortable to you.
4. Bring to mind someone who loves you, and channel their warmth, positive regard, and tenderness. Turn it inward, toward yourself.
5. As you emulate this person, recite loving phrases to yourself, either in your head or out loud, such as "I am safe," "I am worthy," "I am loved," or whatever else feels right and loving.
6. Perform this meditation for at least five minutes, until you feel more at ease.
7. Slowly open your eyes and take one more deep breath.

BUILD YOUR SELF-AWARENESS

If you feel like a stranger within your own skin, it can lead you to overthink, because you can't trust someone you don't really know! This is why building your self-awareness can help you stop overthinking and step into your power.

What to Do

To build up the foundation of who you are, answer the prompt inside each brick on the following page with a fact about yourself. Be honest and curious as you answer.

My favorite physical trait:

How my best friend would describe me:

My biggest fear:

My best quality:

My most annoying habit:

What I would do for work if money and
time didn't matter:

PERFORM A BREATH AWARENESS MEDITATION

Somatic meditation focuses on bringing awareness to the physical; think sensations and bodily awareness. It's all about the mind-body connection as a means of bringing you back to the present moment.

Somatic meditation can be helpful for overthinking. Research has shown that it promotes calm and relaxation.

What to Do

There are several types of somatic meditation. Here, you're going to try a breath awareness somatic meditation. Follow these steps:

1. Go somewhere quiet, with minimal distractions.
2. Sit down and close your eyes.
3. Notice your breathing and how it impacts your body. Do not try to control your breath, do not judge yourself; simply observe how you are breathing. If you're breathing through your nose, focus on the experience of air going in and out of your nostrils. Feel your belly and chest rise and fall. Be at one with your body.
4. Once you feel that you are in a more stable headspace, take one last deep breath in through your nose and out through your mouth. Open your eyes.

VISUALIZE GREATNESS

Overthinking is disempowering. It makes you think the worst of yourself and your abilities. It's the fuel of self-doubt and second-guessing. This is why visualizing yourself accomplishing a major goal can push overthinking to the side and remind you of the real power you possess.

What to Do

Here, you're going to visualize yourself achieving greatness, however *you* define it. Follow these steps:

1. Find somewhere quiet, where you can sit comfortably. Close your eyes.
2. Take five long, deep breaths, paying special attention to your breath.
3. Bring a goal to mind, such as running a marathon, writing a book, buying a house—whatever you're working toward right now.
4. Whatever that goal is, picture yourself accomplishing it. This could be running across the finish line to cheering friends for that marathon, seeing your book on the shelf at the store, or turning the key to the front door of your new home.
5. As you imagine this reality, notice the pride and power rushing through your body. Focus on the sensations of gratitude and self-esteem. Notice what they feel like. Describe the feelings to yourself.
6. Open your eyes and carry those feelings into the rest of your day.

NAME AND DESCRIBE THE FEELING

When you're overwhelmed with emotion, it can be hard to calm down and take the edge off. Overwhelming feelings can intensify your negative thinking and make it even more difficult to stop your thoughts from racing.

Research has shown that naming a strong emotion and describing how it makes you feel can help lessen its intensity and bring you back to a more regulated state. This helps stop overthinking and empowers you.

What to Do

Whenever you're feeling bent out of shape emotionally, turn to this page to describe what you're feeling so you can then name the emotion, lessening its power. For more guidance, check out the first example.

What sensations am I experiencing right now?
I feel weighed down, distracted, and my heart is beating super fast.

What emotion best describes this state?
Anxiety.

What sensations am I experiencing right now?

What emotion best describes this state?

What sensations am I experiencing right now?

What emotion best describes this state?

What sensations am I experiencing right now?

What emotion best describes this state?

What sensations am I experiencing right now?

What emotion best describes this state?

What sensations am I experiencing right now?

What emotion best describes this state?

What sensations am I experiencing right now?

What emotion best describes this state?

RECONNECT WITH YOUR INTUITION WITH MEDITATION

Your intuition is key to living your most authentic possible life. Intuition is your guiding force, your North Star. In other words, your intuition is your instincts—your gut reactions. It's not based in anxiety or fear; it's based on self-trust and knowledge. However, sometimes overthinking causes your inner compass to go askew. Overthinking overrides your instincts and replaces them with nervousness and anxious thoughts. Reconnecting with your intuition helps quiet the noise and get you back to baseline.

What to Do

There are many ways to reconnect with your intuition, and one simple way is through meditation. Just follow these steps:

1. Set a ten-minute timer on your phone.
2. Sit in a comfortable position in a quiet space and close your eyes.
3. Take a deep breath in through your nose. Hold your breath for three seconds. Exhale through your mouth slowly. Repeat this several times, until you are breathing calmly.
4. As you continue to practice your deep breathing, allow whatever it is you're overthinking to enter your mind.
5. Do not cling to the worrisome thought. Instead, whisper or think, "I will figure this out. I trust myself." Repeat this statement as many times as you need, until you feel more self-assured, then open your eyes.

CREATE A PERSONALIZED MORNING ROUTINE

Starting off on the right foot can help the rest of your day go more smoothly, and it can help you avoid overthinking, which can happen when you have too much on your plate. One way to start your day well is by creating a solid morning routine. Having a set routine in place is a form of automation, reducing the number of decisions you need to make and leaving you more headspace for decisions that require more brainpower.

What to Do

Fill in these prompts to create your personalized morning routine! Remember, it's all about what works best for you. If you don't want to wake up at 4 a.m., please don't.

What time I will wake up:

The first thing I will do is:

The second thing I will do is:

The third thing I will do is:

The fourth thing I will do is:

ACKNOWLEDGE YOU CAN'T CHANGE WHAT HAPPENED (AND CONSIDER WHAT YOU CAN DO INSTEAD)

All right: Something unfavorable happened and you're overthinking it to *death*. Maybe you failed a math exam. Maybe a fight with your partner is on your mind. Or maybe a suppressed memory from sixth grade has randomly decided to make a comeback and now you're spiraling about that time when you said the wrong answer with confidence in history class and everyone laughed at you.

Whatever it is you're overthinking, you cannot change what happened. You can't go back in time and study more, avoid the fight, or take back the words you wish you hadn't said. It has happened. It's done. But this should be a relief! Because if it's out of your hands, it should be out of your mind too. That's easier said than done, of course, and that's where this journaling exercise comes into play.

What to Do

On the following page, journal about what happened. Get into the gritty details, the shameful feelings, the utter embarrassment of being alive. Let it all out. Then, once you've made your confession, brainstorm how you can forgive yourself so you can let this thing go. Sure, you can't go back in time. But you can move forward. Think about how:

PRACTICE YOUR MOST SINCERE APOLOGY

Whether you hurt someone's feelings, pissed them off, screwed up at work, or potentially all of the above, you might owe someone an apology. Apologizing can be daunting, so preparing ahead of time can help take the edge off any anxiety you might be experiencing about it.

What to Do

Fill in the blanks to prep for your apology. Be as specific as possible.

Who I need to apologize to:

What happened:

Why I need to apologize:

When I can apologize:

How I can make it right:

How I can forgive myself:

BRAIN DUMP HERE!

Another brain dump session!

What to Do

Simply write down everything that's on your mind. It doesn't have to have any structure, rhyme, or reason. It's about getting all your thoughts out of your mind and onto the page. Go ahead!

BREAK FREE FROM "ANALYSIS PARALYSIS"

Analysis paralysis is a type of overthinking that involves analyzing a problem to the point where you feel completely stuck—unable to move forward in any direction in order to fix the issue.

Analysis paralysis can happen because of emotional overwhelm or because you have way too much information to sort through, preventing you from making your decision.

Luckily, there are various ways you can break free from analysis paralysis, stop overthinking the problem, and get on with your life. In this particular exercise, you're going to break free from analysis paralysis by comparing two options side by side.

What to Do

In the space provided, fill in the prompts to make your way toward a decision.

- What do I need to make a decision about?

  _____

  _____

  _____

- Simply put, what are my two options?

  _____

  _____

  _____

- Pros and cons of option 1:

- Pros and cons of option 2:

- Looking at the pros and cons of each choice side by side, which seems better, and why?

- My choice (and why):

IMAGINE LEAVES ON A STREAM

This visualization exercise is often used in acceptance and commitment therapy (ACT). It's helpful when you're totally overrun by your thoughts and feelings. That's why it's perfect for stopping overthinking!

What to Do

This visualization is easy—just follow these steps:

1. First, get in a comfortable seated position in a quiet space. Once settled, you can either close your eyes or focus your gaze on one spot in the room.
2. Next, imagine yourself sitting next to a gentle stream with leaves slowly floating by on its waves. Pause for ten seconds while you continue imagining the stream.
3. Now, allow your mind to wander and welcome in all types of thoughts, even your overthinking ones.
4. Picture yourself placing each individual thought you have on one of the floating leaves and watching it drift away. This includes soothing, neutral, and anxious thoughts. Let them all go.
5. As your mind clears, stay focused on the stream. Do not rush the stream's flow; allow it to move at its own pace.
6. Whenever your thoughts return, continue placing them on the leaves.
7. When you feel calmer, open your eyes and return to the present moment.

LIST YOUR SAFE PLACES

Feeling safe is a core human need. When you're overthinking, it's usually because you're perceiving some type of threat to your safety and want to stay ahead of it. So it can help to remember what makes you feel safe and secure—and turn to those comforting places when you need refuge from your overactive mind.

What to Do

Here, list your safe places. These can be physical places, such as your bed, your best friend's apartment, or your grandparents' kitchen. You can also list people, activities, shows, movies, songs—anything that makes you feel cozy.

1. _____

2. _____

3. _____

4. _____

5. _____

6. _____

7. _____

8. _____

9. _____

10. _____

PLAY A QUICK-DECISION GAME: THIS OR THAT?

When it comes down to it, decision-making is a skill. If you're constantly waffling over decisions, big and small, try exercising your decision-making muscles with this low-stakes game.

What to Do

Set a timer for two minutes, and answer the this-or-that questions provided here by circling your choice for each matchup. Try to get through the entire list before the timer runs out. Practicing this-or-that games can help you become more decisive, improving your decision-making and problem-solving skills.

- Chocolate or vanilla
- Rolling Stones or Beatles
- Dogs or cats
- Stay up late or go to bed early
- Sleep in or get up early
- Pizza or pasta
- Red or yellow
- Winter or summer
- Ability to fly or ability to read minds
- Hot or cold
- Up or down
- Left or right
- Los Angeles or New York City
- Moon or stars
- Scary movies or romantic comedies
- Ranch or ketchup
- Dance or sing
- Book or TV
- Green or blue
- TikTok or Instagram
- *Jeopardy!* or *Wheel of Fortune*
- Country or hip-hop
- Drive or fly on an airplane
- Paris (France) or Berlin (Germany)
- Harry Potter or Lord of the Rings

ADMIT WHEN YOU'RE PROCRASTINATING

Procrastination is a major sign of overthinking; it's a means of buying more time. It's stalling and avoidance—basically a form of decision paralysis. Calling yourself out when you're procrastinating can help you shift from overthinking to getting things done.

What to Do

Check off anything you're currently experiencing that may indicate you're procrastinating. Once you realize you're putting something off, close this workbook and go face it!

❑   Feeling overwhelmed
❑   Falling into anxious habits
❑   Making excuses
❑   Postponing tasks
❑   Underestimating time
❑   Feeling bored
❑   Setting unrealistic goals

AVOID AVOIDANCE

While you may think that putting off something uncomfortable helps you be more prepared to handle it, that is not always the case. Sometimes "preparing" is just a form of procrastination called avoidance (and it's only holding you back and keeping you stuck).

Avoiding potentially stressful stimuli can actually make the stress response worse, triggering overthinking. This is why facing your fears head-on is vital.

What to Do

It's time to avoid avoidance and face your fears! Follow the prompts on the following page and get honest about your avoidance.

- What I'm avoiding:

  _____

- Why I'm avoiding it:

  _____

  _____

- What emotion am I feeling about this situation?

  _____

  _____

- How is this emotion contributing to my avoidance?

_____

_____

- How can I move forward?

_____

_____

- Deadline for action:

_____

- How I feel after facing the fear:

_____

_____

- What I learned:

_____

_____

TRY THE RAIN TECHNIQUE

The RAIN technique is a great tool for the days you're overwhelmed emotionally. It's a step-by-step exercise that builds self-compassion, and its name is an acronym for its four steps: recognize, allow, investigate, and nurture.

What to Do

Follow the prompts here:

- Recognize what is happening. Describe the thoughts, feelings, and behaviors that are arising within you.
- Allow what you just described to be all that it is, without judgment. Don't try to fix or reframe or do anything about the uncomfortable experiences. Simply allow yourself to feel.
- Investigate the experience. Get curious about why you're reacting or feeling the way you are. Consider what needs you're trying to fulfill.
- Nurture with self-compassion. You can recite self-compassion statements such as "I am okay," or self-validation statements such as "My feelings make sense based on what is going on."

STOP PEOPLE-PLEASING

Did you know that people-pleasing can be a side effect of overthinking? If you didn't, now you do!

When you have a decision to make, especially when it involves others, it's easy to get caught up in worrying about how to make everyone happy. However, you can *never* make everyone happy. It's just not possible! That said, it can still be hard to stop people-pleasing and overthinking. This exercise is here to help.

What to Do

Write yourself a permission slip that gives you the power to be okay with disappointing other people:

EMBRACE UNCERTAINTY

Uncertainty triggers overthinking because the unknown is the *perfect* canvas for what-ifs and worst-case scenarios. And as it turns out, there's actually an evolutionary reason for this. Early on in human history, we needed to continuously scan the horizon (i.e., the unknown) for threats, because we faced the literal threat of death at every turn.

In modern times, we're safer overall than our cave-dwelling ancestors. Our brains haven't caught up to this, however, and out of self-protection they still have the urge to predict what danger could arise next. This can trigger overthinking—and embracing uncertainty and the power of possibility can help stop those spirals of negative thoughts.

What to Do

In this visualization exercise, embrace uncertainty to the fullest. Follow these steps:

1. Find somewhere quiet, where you can sit comfortably without distractions.
2. Once seated, take a few long and deep breaths.
3. Close your eyes and rest your hands, palms facing upward, on your legs or chair.
4. Now imagine an enormous blank canvas in front of you. You're the artist.
5. Stare at the blank canvas for a few moments and picture the infinite variety of ways you could paint it. Channel excitement at the possibility of the masterpiece that is waiting to be created.
6. Once you feel the hope return to your veins, visualize your artist self picking up a paintbrush, dipping it in some paint, and applying it in slow, steady strokes across the canvas. Focus on the motion of the paintbrush only, not so much on what you're painting. Simply enjoy the process of creation, of possibility, and the gentle brushstrokes.

LIST WHAT MAKES YOU HAPPY

When you're overthinking, it's impossible to feel happy. Worries cloud your mind and your perspective becomes skewed, making you believe that you'll never feel okay, safe, and self-assured, ever again. However, this is simply not true. You have been joyous before. You have been at peace before. You have been confident before. You just need a refresher on when those instances were so you can make more room for those feelings to come again (and less space for overthinking).

What to Do

Reminding yourself of what brings you fulfillment can be helpful when overthinking strikes. Not only will it recenter you, but it will also bring your focus away from the overthinking and back to what matters the most. On the following page, list the things that bring you joy, purpose, connection, and fulfillment. Once you have your list, pick something from the list that you can do right at this moment to help stop overthinking.

- [ ]
- [ ]
- [ ]
- [ ]
- [ ]
- [ ]
- [ ]
- [ ]
- [ ]
- [ ]
- [ ]
- [ ]
- [ ]
- [ ]
- [ ]
- [ ]
- [ ]
- [ ]
- [ ]
- [ ]
- [ ]
- [ ]
- [ ]
- [ ]
- [ ]
- [ ]

EXPLAIN WHY PERFECTION IS BORING

Sometimes overthinking can be the result of perfectionism. For example, when you're stuck in the freeze response, it might be because you think you have to be 100 percent "ready" to get going. Or maybe you're so afraid you're not going to do the thing perfectly (a project for work, say) that you'd rather not get started at all—and so you avoid it to prevent the discomfort of your imperfection.

However, perfection is an unrealistic goal. No one is perfect, and no one ever could be. That includes you. Still, this exercise asks you to imagine for a moment that you *could* be perfect—and consider that, even if it were possible, perfection wouldn't be so great.

By thinking and writing about how utterly boring perfection would be, you can free yourself to stop believing it's worth pursuing. Then you can stop overthinking whatever you're mulling over not being perfect—and just accept it for all that it is.

What to Do

Journal about the many reasons why being a perfect person would be incredibly boring. Think about all the ways messiness and mistakes and flaws make for a richer, more connected human experience.

SAY COMFORTING AFFIRMATIONS DURING SHAME FLASHBACKS

Shame is not productive. In fact, it is deeply harmful. When you overthink a scenario where you feel like you messed up or embarrassed yourself (in other words, when you have a shame flashback), the shame tells you that you *are* the mistake you made or the embarrassment you feel.

What to Do

When you're having a shame flashback, recite one or more of the following comforting affirmations to ease that harmful feeling. If nothing stands out to you in this list, use the blank space to write your own soothing affirmations.

- Everyone makes mistakes.
- I don't have to be perfect.
- I am still worthy.
- I matter.
- _____
- _____
- _____
- _____

MAKE TIME FOR QUALITY REST

Rest is imperative for your overall health and well-being. However, resting goes beyond simply relaxing and sleeping. In fact, there are actually seven types of rest:

1. Physical
2. Social
3. Creative
4. Sensory
5. Spiritual
6. Emotional
7. Mental

Making time for quality rest in all of these categories can help you stop overthinking, because it means taking care of yourself and making better, more intentional decisions, which can build your confidence and diminish self-doubt and other things that trigger overthinking.

What to Do

In the following table, you'll find seven rows, each one labeled with one of the types of rest. In each row, reflect on how you are currently including that type of rest, then brainstorm some ways you can infuse more of it into your life. For example, for physical rest, tweak your bedtime routine.

Type of Rest	Current Practices	Improved Practices
Example: Physical	Going to bed at inconsistent times.	Creating a consistent bedtime and sticking to it.
Physical		
Social		
Creative		
Sensory		
Spiritual		
Emotional		
Mental		

THAW THE FREEZE RESPONSE

The freeze response is exactly what it sounds like: You're overwhelmed, and instead of conquering whatever is causing you to freak out, you freeze and do absolutely nothing at all. Instead, you just overthink to the point of paralysis. Thawing the freeze response can help defeat overthinking.

What to Do

Envision yourself frozen in a large ice cube that is preventing you from moving. Breathing in and out slowly, imagine the ice cube melting away slowly. Focus on the dripping water as the ice thaws. When the ice cube has completely melted, envision yourself walking away from where you were frozen and toward the thing you were avoiding.

REFILL YOUR CUP

As you explored in The Basics of Overthinking, sometimes overthinking strikes when you're feeling completely and utterly burned out. Crispy to the point of crumbling. *Done.* When this is the case, it's time to refill your own cup so you can feel better.

What to Do

Take the first step in refilling your cup by listing, in the space provided, five activities that make you feel recharged. Perform one of the activities, then color in part of the water cup, and repeat until it is full.

DE-CATASTROPHIZE YOUR THOUGHTS

Catastrophizing is a classic sign of overthinking. It means considering the worst-case scenario—and blowing the worst-case scenario completely out of proportion. This can include predicting chaotic events becoming reality, or taking painful things that have already happened and ascribing to them the most painful meanings possible.

Some classic examples of catastrophizing include:

- Your breakup is all the evidence you'll ever need that you are unlovable to literally every single person on this planet.
- No one laughed at your joke in the group chat, so it obviously means you're only in the group chat out of pity and no one actually likes you.
- The presentation you're giving at work tomorrow is guaranteed to end in failure, then you'll get fired because your boss will finally see your complete incompetence, and then you won't be able to find another job.

Dramatic? Obviously. But in the moment, the catastrophe you're imagining feels so real and so likely. It can be hard to see reality when you're in the storm that is your mind.

Luckily, you can use this exercise to break free from the catastrophe and stop overthinking the incoming horror movie that would be your life.

What to Do

On the following page, journal the catastrophe you're predicting. Be super specific and honest. Then, write a rebuttal to your prediction and explain why the prediction is unlikely or untrue. For example: "My breakup is not evidence of my worth but a sign that my partner and I weren't the right fit."

FOSTER HEALTHIER RELATIONSHIPS

Your relationships matter. A lot. Research has shown that the people you spend the most time with are directly linked to your health, including your lifespan.

What to Do

Journal about your current relationships and how they make you feel. Be honest about what is working, what isn't working, and how you might improve these relationships. For example, maybe you need better boundaries with a parent, or perhaps you need a little space for a while from a friend who has been constantly negative lately.

COMFORT YOUR INNER CHILD

You may be grown-up, but your inner child is always with you, and they deserve and need your love. An unhealed inner child can cause overthinking, because it's often in childhood that the habit of overthinking develops in the first place. Whether you had critical parents, bullies, or problems with school, you probably began overthinking as a defense mechanism to try to avoid scrutiny and pain.

What to Do

Draw your adult self and your child self, each one near a speech bubble. Then, in your inner child's speech bubble, write what your inner child is worried about. In your adult self's speech bubble, give your inner child a comforting response.

REPLACE ALL-OR-NOTHING THINKING

All-or-nothing thinking is a cognitive distortion in which your thoughts turn directly to absolutes—for example, "I never do anything right" or "Everyone hates me." With all-or-nothing thinking, there is no room for nuance or for the complexity of the human experience. It's a thinking pattern that negatively impacts how you feel about yourself, others, and life in general.

Some classic signs you're engaging in all-or-nothing thinking include:

- Low self-esteem or confidence
- Difficulty with self-compassion
- Anxiety
- Hopelessness
- Feeling like a failure
- Unwillingness to take any sort of risk
- Using words like "always" and "never"

All-or-nothing thoughts can lead to overthinking by encouraging defeatist attitudes, perfectionism, and procrastination. So if you want to stop overthinking, it's useful to replace your all-or-nothing thoughts.

What to Do

On the following page, you're going to replace all-or-nothing thinking with healthier thought patterns. For example:

- All-or-nothing thought: My work is never good enough, so I might as well not even try.
- Replacement thought: There have been various times my work was good enough. I deserve to give this my best shot.

- All-or-nothing thought:
- Replacement thought:

- All-or-nothing thought:
- Replacement thought:

- All-or-nothing thought:
- Replacement thought:

- All-or-nothing thought:
- Replacement thought:

- All-or-nothing thought:
- Replacement thought:

- All-or-nothing thought:
- Replacement thought:

- All-or-nothing thought:
- Replacement thought:

- All-or-nothing thought:
- Replacement thought:

- All-or-nothing thought:
- Replacement thought:

- All-or-nothing thought:
- Replacement thought:

BANISH THE DOOM

As hard as things might feel right now, and as scary as they may seem, you are not doomed. Even if the worst thing that could ever happen does, it will still be okay. If you're not totally convinced of this because all you can see on the horizon is the doom, it's time to banish it.

What to Do

Here, you're going to perform a visualization of banishing the doom. Follow these steps:

1. Find a quiet place where you can sit comfortably.
2. Close your eyes and take a deep breath in and out.
3. Picture a monster named Doom running toward you.
4. As Doom grows closer in your mind's eye, picture yourself becoming bigger and taller.
5. Finally, imagine yourself banishing the approaching Doom by saying, "I do not accept your presence here." Picture Doom turning around and walking away, slumped over in defeat.

FORGIVE YOURSELF FOR BEING HUMAN WITH MEDITATION

Sometimes the most difficult person to forgive is yourself. Whether you're upset over something totally minimal like forgetting the one thing you went to the grocery store for and walking out with a bunch of random impulse buys instead, or even something a little more major, like missing an important deadline at work, the process of letting go of something you did wrong can be super tough.

But no matter how hard it is, you need to forgive yourself anyway. Life is hard enough as it is. Don't make it even harder by being mean to yourself for simply being human.

Self-forgiveness is an important part of stopping overthinking, because if you don't have permission to be wrong, to learn, and to move on, you will fixate on and worry about everything you've ever done and are ever going to do. That's no way to live. You deserve your own grace, and you're going to give yourself that redemption here, through meditation.

What to Do

Follow these steps to perform a self-forgiveness meditation:

1. Find somewhere quiet, without interruptions, where you can sit comfortably and focus.
2. Sit down and close your eyes.
3. Bring awareness to your breath. If it's quick, don't judge yourself; simply slow it down a bit until you are breathing at a calmer, more comfortable pace.
4. Continue to breathe in and out intentionally. As you inhale, think, "All I can ever be is human." As you exhale, think, "I forgive myself."
5. Repeat these affirmations and deep breaths five times.

DO WHAT WORKED IN THE PAST

Let's face it: You're feeling insecure right now. Anxious. Not your best. Worried about *everything*. When you begin to feel this way, it can be hard to remember that these feelings are temporary—that you will feel better again, not only because that's the nature of emotions, but also because you know how to self-regulate.

When you can't decide what to try to do to feel better, it's helpful to remember that this is not your first rodeo. You've been sad before; you've been anxious before; you've been heartbroken before. You just need to recall what you did that helped in the past, because it's likely to help now too.

What to Do

Either in the space provided, or on a separate piece of paper, reflect on a time when you've felt this way before. Then remember what you did to get through that tough time. Consider what wasn't very helpful and what *did* work. Once you've journaled about this, you'll likely see some strategies you can use right here, right now, to face the current situation.

DO A QUICK BODY SCAN

Performing a scan of how each part of your body feels can help recenter you and help you ground yourself in the present moment rather than worrying about the future or ruminating on the past.

What to Do

Follow these steps and feel the stress leave your body:

1. Find a quiet place where you can sit comfortably.
2. Close your eyes.
3. Pick a specific body part to begin with, such as the top of your head or your toes.
4. Wherever you chose, focus on that area and how it feels. Observe any sensations, uncomfortable or otherwise, for twenty seconds. Be nonjudgmental; simply notice them.
5. Once the twenty seconds are up, move on to the next body part and repeat.
6. Repeat until you've scanned your whole body.

QUIT YOUR FORTUNE-TELLING CAREER

Here's the thing: You're not a fortune teller. Or maybe you're trying to be, but how is it working for you? Likely not great, and that's okay! The future is full of uncertainty, and while that fact can be scary, it is also exciting. It's time to move on from trying to predict how things will unfold and find a better use of your mind.

What to Do

Write your letter of resignation from fortune-telling. Explain why you're quitting and what you're moving on to instead.

WRITE PERSONALIZED SELF-EMPOWERMENT STATEMENTS

Whatever it is you're spiraling about, you've got this. You really do—even if you feel like everything that can go wrong is and will. Being in a self-defeating mindset makes you more vulnerable to overthinking tendencies. This is why it's so important to remind yourself of your own strength. You can do this through self-empowerment statements.

What to Do

Fill in the blanks here to create personalized self-empowerment statements. At the end, write your own self-empowerment statements. Return to these statements whenever self-doubt creeps into your mind.

- Even though I'm feeling _____ [current emotion], I am still going to get through this.
- I have my own back, because _____ _____.
- Life is hard, but I am _____ [positive attributes about yourself].
- I am stronger than _____.
- I will be okay because _____.
- _____
- _____
- _____
- _____
- _____
- _____

NOTICE GLIMMERS

A glimmer is the opposite of a trigger. Basically, glimmers are little things that make you feel safe, happy, or delighted. Luckily, glimmers can be found every single day and can help you feel more grounded, grateful, and frankly, sane—all deterrents for overthinking!

What to Do

In each star, write down any recent glimmers you have had. For example, you got to pet a cute dog on your morning walk. Or you finally got ahold of your best friend after three days of phone tag and had the best conversation ever.

PUT THE PROBLEM ON THE SHELF

When you're mentally exhausted, it can make problem-solving all the more difficult and overthinking all the easier to turn to. This is why taking a step back and giving your mind a rest can help you stop overthinking.

What to Do

Follow these steps to visualize putting your problem aside until you're ready to take it on in a calmer, clearer state of mind:

1. Find somewhere quiet and sit down.
2. Slowly take a few deep breaths in and out.
3. Once you're settled, close your eyes and visualize a shelf above you.
4. Imagine yourself walking to the shelf while holding a box that contains your problem.
5. Picture yourself placing the box on the shelf and walking away from it.
6. When you feel ready to conquer your problem, imagine walking back to the shelf and taking the problem back down. With time and space, you'll be far better equipped to handle that problem!

IDENTIFY YOUR PERSONAL VALUES

Knowing yourself not only fosters more self-trust—it also helps you lead a more aligned, fulfilling life. And when you know you're living a life that is truly a reflection of you, you're less likely to overthink your choices. You know you've got your own back, and you always figure things out.

One way to get to know yourself better is by identifying your personal values. Personal values are the pillars of your individual belief system and what you consider to be the most important things in life.

Some examples of common personal values include:

- Generosity
- Family
- Gratitude
- Bravery
- Integrity
- Kindness
- Health
- Honesty
- Dependability
- Achievement
- Creativity
- Adventure
- Faith
- Love
- Respect
- Independence
- Friendship
- Balance

What to Do

Write down your top five values, why you care about each one so much, and how you can live up to these values:

Value 1:

- Why I care:
- How I can live up to this value:

Value 2:

- Why I care:
- How I can live up to this value:

Value 3:

- Why I care:
- How I can live up to this value:

Value 4:

- Why I care:
- How I can live up to this value:

Value 5:

- Why I care:
- How I can live up to this value:

COLOR THIS RELAXING SUNSET SCENE

It's time to color again! This time, it's a sunset scene, symbolizing that you're done with overthinking. What's done is done, and it's time to move on!

What to Do

Sit back and color in the sunset scene. Remember: Focus only on the act of coloring. When the overthinking thoughts pop up—and they will—invite yourself back to the present moment and focus on the relaxing scene.

ANSWER THESE OVERTHINKING QUESTIONS

Does what you're overthinking really require the amount of mental energy you're putting toward it? If you're unsure, this is the perfect exercise for you, because it will help you realize it definitely doesn't!

What to Do

Answer the following questions related to whatever it is you're overthinking. You'll come to realize that what you're so worried about is probably not as big a deal as it seems right now.

- Will this matter tomorrow?

- Will this matter next week?

- Will this matter next year? In five years?

- What can I control, if anything?

- What is absolutely out of my hands?

LIST THINGS YOU NEED TO LET GO OF IN LIFE

The more you release, the more room you have to focus on what matters. When you focus on what matters, you lessen overthinking, because you're operating with a clearer mind. Not everything needs to be held on to. It's time to figure out what you need to let go of.

What to Do

List everything you want to let go of in your life. You can list things that are big or small, tangible or more conceptual. For example, you could let go of people-pleasing, your history report from seventh grade that you've been holding on to just in case you need it later, your situationship's phone number in your phone, or anything else that you no longer need.

I LET GO OF . . .

- [ ]
- [ ]
- [ ]
- [ ]
- [ ]
- [ ]
- [ ]
- [ ]
- [ ]
- [ ]
- [ ]
- [ ]
- [ ]
- [ ]
- [ ]
- [ ]
- [ ]
- [ ]
- [ ]
- [ ]
- [ ]
- [ ]

ENTER YOUR DO-NOT-DISTURB ERA

Unbothered. That is exactly how you're about to feel because you're about to enter your do-not-disturb era. Basically, you're taking the power back from overthinking by deciding you're just not going to let it bother you.

What to Do

Enter your do-not-disturb era through meditation. Follow these steps:

1. Get in a comfortable position in a quiet room and close your eyes. You can sit or lie down—whatever is comfortable and will help you focus.
2. Bring awareness to your breath (how shallow it is, whether you are breathing through your nose or mouth, where it moves in your body).
3. Start breathing deeply, slowly inhaling through your nose and slowly exhaling through your mouth.
4. As you breathe, think the following affirmation: "I am not concerned with things that I cannot control." Keep repeating this affirmation until you feel more at peace, then open your eyes.

FIND CREATIVE HOBBIES YOU LOVE

While it's always helpful to have various creative tasks to do to distract yourself from overthinking, a regular creative practice in the form of a hobby is even better! Here, you're going to find a creative hobby to pick up when overthinking strikes.

What to Do

Write down some creative hobbies you're interested in pursuing—for example, learning the guitar, taking up painting, or trying pottery. Use this page to brainstorm ways you can pursue one or more of these hobbies: finding local community centers that offer classes, following YouTube tutorials, or other ways to experiment and learn.

TRY THIS WEEK-LONG DECLUTTER CHALLENGE

People say a cluttered home usually indicates a cluttered mind, and that makes total sense. After all, research has shown that clutter is associated with higher levels of stress. That said, decluttering can also feel overwhelming—it's easy to overthink what you want to keep and what to get rid of. But the end result is worth the trouble! And the decluttering process itself can ward off over-thinking by giving you valuable practice in decision-making and self-trust.

What to Do

Declutter your home to clear space in your mind. In this chart, write down what you're decluttering and why.

Day of the Week	What I Decluttered and Why

GO FROM ASHAMED TO GRATEFUL

Gratitude is an act of mindfulness that can be helpful when you're experiencing shame for acting in a way you aren't too proud of, such as forgetting to text a friend back or missing an important deadline at work. Your first instinct might be to apologize in a way that is self-defeating ("I'm such a screw-up," "I understand if you don't trust me anymore," etc.). However, an expression of gratitude helps everyone feel better!

What to Do

Write about times you weren't your best self and offer an apology that is shame-focused. For example, if it's a missed work deadline: "I'm sorry I am so behind and messed everything up." Next, rewrite the shame-based apology to one of appreciation, for example: "Thanks to the team for your patience and support as I catch up."

Shameful moment:

_____

- Shame-based apology: _____
- Grateful apology: _____

Shameful moment:

_____

- Shame-based apology: _____
- Grateful apology: _____

LIST YOUR SUCCESSES

It's time to give yourself some well-deserved praise, and you can do this by listing your successes, big and small and everything in between and beyond. You are more capable than you are giving yourself credit for being. Reminding yourself of your power can help protect that power from your woes of uncertainty and fears of imperfection or failure.

What to Do

In the award ribbons provided, write down some of your most recent successes. A success doesn't have to be a major win; it can be as simple as not sleeping past your alarm!

IDENTIFY THE ROOT WORRY THROUGH JOURNALING

Overthinking is rarely only *caused* by the event you're ruminating on. More often, a deeper worry is at the root of your fixation on a certain topic or situation.

For example, perhaps you're overthinking something that happened in the past, such as a bad first date where you feel like you said every possible wrong thing there was to say. This memory may resurface whenever you're feeling that you're too much to ever really be loved and that cringey date was a prime example of this "fact."

What to Do

Use the following page to get curious about the root worry tied to your over-thinking so you can address it head-on. First, write down the subject or event you're overthinking. Then write what root worry you're ascribing to the situation. Once you have that root worry, ponder why this is not the case at all with self-compassion, reality checks, or whatever feels best to help you feel better.

So to use the first date as an example: The memory of the awkward dinner date is making you feel sad, lonely, and ashamed, and these feelings are making you doubt yourself and worry you will never find someone. In fact, you are using this painful memory as evidence of being unlovable. And being unlovable is a huge root worry for you across the board. Now that you recognize this, you can see that a bad first date is just that, and not an indictment of your worth. Everyone has less-than-ideal dates; it's just part of the game of life!

LET THE SPIRAL GO

Visualization is a powerful anti-anxiety hack that helps bring you back to the present moment and out of the land of worst-case scenarios. Here, you're going to visualize the spiral of overthinking you're experiencing—and then let it go.

What to Do

Follow the steps to complete this exercise:

1. Close your eyes and visualize a tornado heading your way.
2. Picture it picking up all of your anxious thoughts and making them swirl in its vortex.
3. Just as the tornado is about to grab you, step aside.
4. Watch the spiral spin away and out of your life.

LISTEN TO YOUR MIND, BODY, AND SOUL

Meditation is a great way to combat overthinking. It calms you down, and it helps you increase your self-awareness and be more mindful about your life. Here, you're going to perform a mind, body, and soul meditation.

What to Do

Listen to your mind, body, and soul through meditation using the following steps:

1. Go to a quiet room and get in a comfortable position, either sitting or lying down. Close your eyes.
2. Bring awareness to your breath. Observe the speed of your breath and whether you're mostly breathing through your nose or mouth.
3. Begin breathing more deeply in through your nose and out through your mouth.
4. As you practice deep breathing, turn your attention to your mind and ask it what it needs. Listen to its response.
5. Next, turn your attention to your body and ask it what it needs. Listen to its response.
6. Finally, turn your attention to your soul and ask it what it needs. Listen to its response.
7. Once you have your answers, open your eyes and go do what your mind, body, and soul are asking you to do!

CONQUER TASK PARALYSIS

Task paralysis is similar to analysis paralysis, but it's more about not knowing where to start when it comes to your tasks. This happens when you have so much to do that you have the freeze response, becoming literally unable to do anything on your seemingly never-ending to-do list. Luckily, you *can* break free from being unsure of where to start and just get the ball rolling. And that's exactly what you're going to do here!

What to Do

On the following page, conquer your task paralysis by rewriting your to-do list. First, write down everything that you have to do, big and small. Once you've made your overwhelming list, set a timer for ten minutes. During this time, narrow your to-do list down to three to five priorities that must be done *today*. Once the ten-minute timer goes off, start with the first of your top priorities. Completing that one will motivate you to conquer the rest!

My To-Do List:

My Top Priorities:

IMAGINE A FLICKERING CANDLE TO CALM YOUR MIND

Sometimes, overthinking leads to a state of complete anxiety and paralysis. It can be hard to calm down when overthinking gets this strong. This is where visualization comes in; visualization is a great tool for calming your mind and stopping overthinking.

What to Do

Follow these steps to perform a calming visualization:

1. Find somewhere quiet, where you can sit comfortably.
2. Close your eyes.
3. Start breathing deeply, paying special attention to the rise and fall of your chest as you breathe in through your nose and out through your mouth.
4. As you become more relaxed, bring to mind a serene room with a cozy pile of pillows and blankets in the middle, surrounded by flickering candles.
5. As you picture this scene, imagine yourself settling into that relaxing spot.
6. Look around the room in your mind and focus on the candlelight. You can focus on one candle in particular and take note of its shape, movement, and scent. Or you can focus on the shadows the candles make on the walls.
7. Feel your body relax more and more and your anxiety burn out as you focus on this visualization.
8. Perform this visualization for five to ten minutes, or however long it takes for you to feel less stressed.

WRITE YOUR DAILY SELF-CARE CHECKLIST

When you're busy, burned out, and totally at your wits' end, self-care often falls to the wayside. However, self-care isn't just important; it's absolutely *necessary* for keeping yourself happy, healthy, and fulfilled.

What to Do

Write a daily self-care checklist to help keep your self-care game strong. Include all the nonnegotiable self-care tasks you can't put off—for example, brushing your teeth, washing your face, taking medication, or engaging in movement.

❏ _____

❏ _____

❏ _____

❏ _____

❏ _____

❏ _____

❏ _____

❏ _____

❏ _____

❏ _____

❏ _____

❏ _____

❏ _____

❏ _____

❏ _____

PLAY SELF-LOVE BINGO

Self-love is essential. It is the foundation of self-care and living a healthy, fulfilled life. However, sometimes practicing self-love is easier said than done, especially when you're overthinking. After all, overthinking is all tangled up with self-doubt and anxiety.

When you're noticing overthinking starting to take over your mind, self-love can help bring you back to the present and slow everything down. If you're struggling with how to practice self-love, then it's time to play self-love bingo!

What to Do

On the following page, you'll see a bingo board with eleven different self-love practices you can engage in right now to improve your mood, boost your self-esteem, and practice self-care. In the free space, get creative and come up with a personalized way to show yourself some love. After you complete each exercise, X out the box.

After you've completed the board, write down how you feel and, in the lines beneath the board, reflect on why loving yourself is so important.

Self-Love Bingo

Take a relaxing shower.	Practice gentle movement.	Journal.
Phone a friend.	Free Space:	Take a 15-minute break.
Do something fun.	Recite positive affirmations.	Breathe deeply.
Drink water.	Eat a healthy snack.	Meditate.

Self-love is crucial because:

_____

_____

_____

_____

_____

_____

WRITE A LETTER FROM YOUR HIGHEST SELF

Your highest self already exists. In fact, they're within you! However, when you're in a spiral of overthinking, it's hard to listen to your highest self (a.k.a. the best, most confident and self-assured version of you). Luckily, there are ways you can tune out the noise and find out what your higher self has to say. Here's one way: Write a letter from your highest self to the current you.

What to Do

Write a letter from the perspective of your highest self. Tell your current self how much better things get, how much more at peace you will feel, and that it's going to be okay even though everything feels unmanageable right now.

TRY OPPOSITE ACTION

The idea of opposite action comes from dialectical behavioral therapy (DBT). It's known as an emotional regulation skill—basically a strategy for calming yourself down when you're in a panic. This skill requires you to check in with whatever emotion you're experiencing and do the opposite of what it's begging you to do. Opposite action can be especially helpful during shame spirals. For example, if you want to self-isolate, the opposite action would be to call a friend.

What to Do

Fill in the blanks when overthinking:

1. Identify the emotion you feel right now: _____

2. What is the emotion asking you to do?

   _____

3. What opposite action can you take?

   _____

4. How did it go?

   _____

MAP YOUR PLAN OF ATTACK

Overthinking can make solving problems feel impossible. This is because being in a more anxious state makes decision-making tougher. It can be tricky to understand what you need to do next when emotions are high and your mind is racing.

If you're currently overthinking some sort of problem and you aren't sure what step to take next (or where to even start) map your plan of attack by journaling.

What to Do

On the following page, journal about the problem at hand, and then write directions for three routes you could take to solve the issue. Once you've mapped out three routes, decide which one makes the most sense, and take that route to make things better.

The Problem:

_____

_____

_____

Route 1:

_____

_____

_____

Route 2:

_____

_____

_____

Route 3:

_____

_____

_____

WHAT DO YOU WISH YOU'D DONE DIFFERENTLY?

It's okay if you didn't live up to your own standards. It's actually a great learning opportunity and a chance to do better next time. Reflecting on what you wish you had done differently in a given situation is also an awesome way to get to know yourself and your values better—which helps diminish triggers for overthinking, such as self-doubt.

What to Do

Here, get honest with yourself about a situation where you didn't live up to your own expectations. This honesty doesn't have to be brutal in order to be effective. As it turns out, self-compassion will help you move on and move upward more than any self-deprecation or negative self-talk ever could.

Write about what happened, and share what you wish you had done differently. Then turn the page and let it go!

RELEASE SHAME ABOUT THE PAST

What's done is done. You deserve to let it go and put it down. And if you're struggling to let go, meditation can help you release shame about the past and move forward.

What to Do

Follow these steps to perform a meditation to release shame:

1. Find somewhere quiet, where you can sit comfortably. Close your eyes.
2. Bring awareness to your breath. If it's quick, slow it down.
3. Once breathing at a comfortable pace, bring the shame-inducing event to mind.
4. As you inhale, think, "What's done is done."
5. As you exhale, think, "I release this shame."
6. Repeat five times until the shame fades away.

DECIDE BETWEEN SOLUTION-FOCUSED COPING AND EMOTION-FOCUSED COPING

If you have a problem and aren't sure how to face it, it can be helpful to know whether you need to take action or find another way to feel better. In other words, it's helpful to decide between solution-focused coping and emotion-focused coping.

Solution-focused coping is concerned with doing something to fix a problem, while emotion-focused coping is all about regulating your emotional response to whatever is causing you problems. When you know which one to use in a given situation, you can handle your problem more effectively and avoid overthinking.

What to Do

Write down your problem, and then list possible emotion-focused and solution-focused ways it can be conquered. Keep in mind that there may also be options that require both your active participation and feeling-focused strategies. For example, you're angry at a friend and are dreading the confrontation. The emotion-focused coping strategy would be to give yourself time to cool off before the discussion. The solution-focused coping would be to write down exactly what you want to tell your friend when you talk. The "both" part of this would be to schedule a time when you feel emotionally safe to chat. Which ones seem most helpful at this time? Once you have your answers, you can face the problem head-on.

Solution-Focused   Emotion-Focused
                Both

TALK TO YOURSELF LIKE YOU ARE YOUR OWN BFF

Think about it like this: If you talked to your closest friends the same way you sometimes talk to yourself, they would likely no longer want to be your friends. So why be so mean to yourself? Here, you're going to stop a shame spiral by replacing that mean voice in your head with the voice of your BFF talking you through it.

What to Do

Follow these prompts:

- Your BFF's name: _____
- What the shame spiral is about: _____
- Why it's going to be okay: _____
- Comforting affirmation: _____

LIST YOUR WARNING SIGNS OF IMPENDING OVERTHINKING

Before the storm of overthinking rolls into your mind, you can prepare for the downpour by understanding the signs that the weather's changing. Being aware of your warning signs can help you manage stress in the moment and even stop the spiral altogether.

What to Do

List the signs that warn you you're heading for overthinking. These might include lack of self-care, irritability, exhaustion, or sleep issues.

-
-
-
-
-
-

AUDIT YOUR SOCIAL MEDIA FEEDS

You live in the digital age, meaning your online life bleeds into your real life. Social media can be a great tool for connecting with other people and expressing yourself, but doomscrolling and comparison traps can also be a source of a lot of stress and anxiety. Your social media feeds might be minefields of overthinking hazards—but they don't have to be! Diminish the risk of overthinking by auditing your social media feeds so you only follow and interact with accounts that are beneficial to you.

What to Do

List any and all social media platforms you have an account on. Reflect on how each account makes you feel, and figure out how you can have a more positive experience on each one.

Social Platform: _____

- How it makes me feel: _____
- Do I need to unfollow or mute any accounts? _____
  (If yes, check off when done.)

Social Platform: _____

- How it makes me feel: _____
- Do I need to unfollow or mute any accounts? _____
  (If yes, check off when done.)

Social Platform:

- How it makes me feel:
- Do I need to unfollow or mute any accounts?
  (If yes, check off when done.)

Social Platform:

- How it makes me feel:
- Do I need to unfollow or mute any accounts?
  (If yes, check off when done.)

Social Platform:

- How it makes me feel:
- Do I need to unfollow or mute any accounts?
  (If yes, check off when done.)

COLOR THIS MANDALA

Another coloring activity! Here, you're going to color in a mandala. A mandala is a circular shape containing beautiful geometric designs. From the Sanskrit word for "circle" or "center," mandalas are used in various spiritual followings including Hinduism, Buddhism, Jainism, and Shinto to help with meditative practices.

What to Do

Color the mandala. As your anxious thoughts roll in, bring yourself back to the moment by bringing your attention back to coloring and coloring only. You can even narrate your process to interrupt potential spirals. For example: "I am coloring this section pink. Now I am coloring the next section yellow."

IGNORE TOXIC POSITIVITY WITH MEDITATION

Yes, being positive is great. But when it turns toxic? Not so much. Maybe you're struggling with something relationally or personally at work or school, so you tried talking to a loved one about your hurt—and they responded with something along the lines of "At least . . . " or "You just have to be positive!" Did you feel dismissed or even embarrassed for opening up about the pain? If so, that's toxic positivity at work.

Toxic positivity—pressure to only express positive feelings—is unrealistic, because no one can be happy all the time. Life is hard. Painful things happen, and you need to experience the pain to move through it and past it. Don't overthink the fact that you "should" be positive right now. You're not. You're hurting, and that's okay.

What to Do

Here, you're going to ignore toxic positivity and validate your experience through meditation.

1. Find somewhere quiet, where you can sit comfortably.
2. Close your eyes and start breathing deeply in through your nose and out through your mouth.
3. As you breathe, focus on your breath.
4. As you inhale, think, "My pain is valid and makes sense."
5. As you exhale, think, "I give myself permission to feel what I do, without judgment."
6. Take four more slow breaths, repeating these affirmations each time, then open your eyes.

REMEMBER TO THANK YOUR PAST SELF

Your past self has made a lot of mistakes; this is definitely true. But instead of feeling shame about and fixating on missteps, it is far more productive to be kind to your past self. If you're bristling at that concept, this is the perfect exercise for you; it's time to *thank* the person you were in the past.

Here's the thing: You wouldn't be who you are today without your former self. They shaped you. They taught you. They carried you to this present moment, even in all their imperfect, flawed ways. That is something to be admired. That is something they deserve to be thanked for.

What to Do

On the following page, write a letter to your past self and thank them for everything they did for you. You can refer to a specific scenario that you are overthinking, such as a bad first date or a fight with your best friend. You can also just write a general letter of gratitude. Write whatever feels authentic to you.

Your past self deserves your love. Show them that.

Dear Past Self,

Love, Your Future Self

BE IN THE PRESENT MOMENT WITH MEDITATION

Being in the present moment can help you stop overthinking, because it takes you out of thinking about the scary future or ruminating on the painful past and puts you in the here and now: the only moment you really have power over. This ultimately will help calm you down.

What to Do

Meditation is one of the best ways to step back into the moment at hand. Follow these steps to bring yourself back to the present moment through meditation:

1. Set a ten-minute timer.
2. Find a comfortable position in a quiet area. You can either sit or lie down on the floor, in your bed, on a chair—whatever works! Once settled, close your eyes.
3. Take a deep breath in through your nose. Hold your breath for three seconds, then exhale through your mouth slowly. Repeat this several times, until you are breathing calmly.
4. As you continue to practice your deep breathing, allow whatever it is you're overthinking to enter your mind.
5. Do not cling to the worrisome thought. Instead, whisper or think, "I can only be here right now. I return to the present moment." Keep repeating this phrase until you feel at ease. Open your eyes.

IMAGINE BEING YOUR CALMEST SELF

Somewhere within you is someone who is cool, calm, and collected. Seriously! You've just lost touch with them is all. But that's okay; you can reconnect with your inner calm through visualization.

Reconnecting with your inner calm can help diminish overthinking because the clearer your mind and heart are, the less likely you are to question and doubt yourself and your choices.

What to Do

You're going to imagine being your calmest self. Before performing this visualization exercise, find somewhere quiet, where you can sit comfortably and uninterrupted. Once you're settled, follow these steps:

1. Close your eyes and take three deep breaths in through your nose and out through your mouth.
2. Imagine yourself in a situation that usually causes you stress. Maybe it's going on a first date, taking a test, or asking your boss for time off.
3. Once you have your scenario, imagine showing up as your calmest, most self-assured self. What would you say, how would you regulate your nerves, and how would you own what you needed?
4. Notice how you feel when you imagine this version of yourself. Pay attention to your body as well as your emotions and mental state as you start to feel calmer and more collected.
5. Open your eyes and channel this calm version of yourself into your reality.

EXPRESS GRATITUDE FOR THE PRESENT MOMENT

Gratitude is a true practice of mindfulness and grounding yourself in the here and now. Being grateful is an act of humility, of appreciation, and of tender awareness.

Gratitude is also linked to many mental health benefits, including better sleep, improved mood, greater empathy, lessened negativity, and enhanced self-esteem.

Gratitude can be helpful to stop overthinking in particular because it brings your attention to the present, to the positive, and to love. Overthinking has no place here!

What to Do

On the following page, you're going to express everything you're grateful for in this present moment. You can reference the great lunch you had; you can think about how you got some good sleep for once last night; you can consider the fact you have so many people who love you and have your back. Whatever comes to mind right here, right now, write it down.

APPENDIX

In addition to the activities in this workbook, you may want to check out more resources as you tackle your overthinking. The following are organizations, publications, and other tools that can help you take your power back and improve your overall mental health:

- **National Alliance on Mental Illness (NAMI):** The largest grassroots mental health organization in the United States, NAMI works to increase mental health awareness, provide support, and educate communities. Get tips on mental health management and find educational resources, support groups, and more at NAMI.org.

- **Substance Abuse and Mental Health Services Administration (SAMHSA):** An agency within the U.S. Department of Health and Human Services, SAMHSA is dedicated to improving mental and behavioral health in the United States. Find treatment, educational resources, and more on their website at SAMHSA.gov.

- *Verywell Mind*: This is a fantastic website centered around mental health, wellness, and relationships. Find expert and research-backed tips on stopping overthinking, stress management techniques, and more at VerywellMind.com.

- *The Mighty*: *The Mighty* is a mental health community and publication all in one. Find helpful information and feel less alone at TheMighty.com.

- *Psychology Today:* Beyond articles on a variety of topics, *Psychology Today* has a directory where you can search for a therapist based on a variety of factors, including location, health insurance, areas of expertise, and more. It's all at PsychologyToday.com.

- **HelpGuide.org:** An independent nonprofit, HelpGuide.org is one of the world's leading mental health publications, providing valuable education, tools, resources, and advice for living well. Check it out at HelpGuide.org.

- **Headspace:** Headspace is a one-stop mental health app that provides mindfulness tools, mental health coaching, guided meditations, and more. Learn more at Headspace.com.

ABOUT THE AUTHOR

Molly Burford is a writer and pro overthinker who covers relationships, mental health, and authenticity. Her work has appeared in *Allure*, *Glamour*, and *Self*, among others. She is the author of *The No Worries Workbook*, *Say Yes to Yourself*, *Moments to Hold Close*, and *DIY Bucket List*. Molly was born and raised in metro Detroit, where she currently lives with her dog, Bruce.